THE ARCHITECTURE
OF DEMOCRACY

THE ARCHITECTURE OF DEMOCRACY

AMERICAN ARCHITECTURE AND THE LEGACY OF THE REVOLUTION

ALLAN GREENBERG

FOREWORD BY GEORGE P. SHULTZ

RIZZOLI
NEW YORK

First published in the United States of America in 2006 by
RIZZOLI INTERNATIONAL PUBLICATIONS, INC.
300 Park Avenue South, New York, NY 10010
www.rizzoliusa.com

ISBN-10: 0-8478-2793-3
ISBN-13: 9-78084-78279-30
LCCN: 2006921406

Designed by Abigail Sturges

Printed and bound in China

2006 2007 2008 2009 2010/ 10 9 8 7 6 5 4 3 2 1

FRONT COVER
The Lady Pepperrell House (1760), Kittery Point Maine (p. 35)

BACK COVER
*The Mall in Washington, D.C., with the Washington Monument in
the foreground and the U.S. Capitol in the background (p. 11)*

ENDPAPERS
*Perspective drawing of Girard College, Philadelphia, designed
by Thomas U. Walters (pp. 98–99)*

PREVIOUS PAGES
*The Great Seal Capital for the State Department designed by the
Author for the Secretary of State's office (1985) and the new
Treaty Ceremony Room (1986)*

*View of Richmond in 1798 painted by Benjamin Henry Latrobe.
Jefferson's white capitol dominates the town of "not more than
700 houses."*

PAGE 204
View of the sixth Virginia Statehouse (p. 91)

CONTENTS

ACKNOWLEDGMENTS

Like my book *George Washington, Architect*, this volume is a speculative essay that explores certain unresolved aspects of American architectural history and current architectural practice. My central concern is the ways in which American architecture embodies the precepts outlined in the founding documents of the Republic. I am not an architectural historian, and am aware that I have not described all of the profound connections between the political world of seventeenth- and eighteenth-century England—with her amazingly rich vernacular architectural tradition—and colonial and federal America. My point of view is that of a practicing architect. I use buildings to bridge the gaps where textual documentation does not exist or is inadequate. Although they may be difficult to read, buildings tell stories through their form, symbolic content, and relationship to the surrounding city.

I am deeply indebted to many people, teachers, colleagues, and scholars whose books, articles, conversations, and criticisms have been of vital importance to me. Some have been patient enough to listen to my ideas and comment on their shortcomings over the long period of their gestation. In particular, I acknowledge debts of gratitude to Vincent J. Scully, Carroll William Westfall, William L. MacDonald, James D. and Georgianna Kornwolf, Mark Allan Hewitt, and Witold Rybczynski, all of whom are leaders in their particular fields. The late Sir John Summerson offered valuable advice in the early stages when I was struggling to define my outline, and Sandra Vitzthum generously shared her insights on my preoccupation with the idea of anthropomorphism. I remain indebted to my associate Thomas Noble, who over the years thoughtfully responded to my tedious requests for comments on drafts of parts of the text, and to my son and fellow architect, Peter Greenberg, for the difficult questions he invariably raised. I also thank the architects in my office, who generously shared their ideas and experiences with me.

I want to acknowledge my indebtedness to Dennis Durden, a remarkable teacher and visiting professor in Yale's City Planning Department, who convinced me of the ecological relationship of architecture and the world around us, and to the late Honorable John P. Cotter, Chief Justice of Connecticut, for asking me a question in 1967 that I have spent the rest of my life trying to answer: Why were architects of the past routinely able to design wonderful courthouses while contemporary practice seems to produce courthouses many judges consider unsatisfactory?

My skilled research assistant and librarian, Patricia Price, and my editors Mimi Harrison and Melissa Weisberg, kept me focused on the straight and narrow, challenging me with my own motto: There is always a better way. Without the patience, persistence, and good eye of my associate Diana Apalategui, this book's illustrations would be fewer and of less interest. Special thanks to Wade Zimmerman, Robert Lautman, and numerous other photographers who always responded to my last minute requests for yet another photograph.

My old friend David Morton, architecture editor at Rizzoli International Publications, suggested that the short text I was developing as a television program would also be an interesting book. I am thankful for his patience, good humor, and generosity of spirit. Douglas Curran, also at Rizzoli, wisely and tactfully guided this book through the tedious process of design, layout, and editing. Abigail Sturges designed the wonderful layout.

And a particular debt of gratitude is owed to my wife, the painter Judith Seligson, who patiently endured what must have seemed like endless years of discussion about the ideas in this book. At crisis points, she was always able to reformulate problems into a more manageable form and to suggest alternate avenues of exploration. It was Judy and our friend Roba Whiteley who suggested I take ideas we were discussing over dinner and develop them into a television program about architecture.

To all these people I acknowledge that many of the most fruitful ideas in this book were honed with the help of their insights. Of course, the mistakes are all mine.

FOREWORD

AMERICA'S REVOLUTIONARY ARCHITECTURE OF DEMOCRACY

GEORGE SHULTZ

Allan Greenberg has given us the eyes to see what is around us. He reminds us that architecture is culture. Architecture tells us who we are, what we are thinking, and how we regard ourselves. I had the great privilege of working with this eminent architect as he redesigned the suite of offices on the seventh floor of the U.S. State Department used by the Secretary and Deputy Secretary of State. This included transforming five nondescript reception rooms that connected two elevator lobbies into the Treaty Ceremony Suite. He brought excitement and he brought meaning to what had been drab and meaningless, though in some ways grand, spaces. Allan succeeded the late Edward Vason Jones, who redesigned most of the eighth floor diplomatic reception rooms in a previous decade.

I can recall many occasions when I took foreign dignitaries to events in these wonderful rooms. I would show them the desk that Thomas Jefferson designed and built and on which he wrote portions of our Declaration of Independence. The message was: We have a great history and part of our history is a Renaissance man who was secretary of state, president, and also a gifted architect, designer of furniture, and even a carpenter. The brilliance of his writing gave special meaning to the desk and the desk, in turn, eased Jefferson into his productivity. The grace and elegance of the offices, meeting rooms, and diplomatic reception rooms provide a setting in which Jefferson's small writing desk and the words written there take on an immense, even universal, significance. As you look around these rooms, other names join Jefferson's: Adams, Franklin, Madison, Monroe, Jay—our founding fathers, as well as, more recently, George Marshall.

The lines in the rooms are clean and classic, with graceful columns that recall the democratic striving of Greek and Roman antiquity that the founders had so intensely studied. Yet Allan Greenberg's designs, while classic, are also originals, reflecting the way in which classical political thought and practice were naturalized and improved upon to meet the needs of a new, modern nation on American soil. Simple elegance is a theme.

The architectural redesign and rebuilding of the eighth floor diplomatic reception rooms was incomplete when I took office as Secretary of State and I was delighted to restart the program and to be part of the new Franklin, Monroe, and Madison rooms. Next in line to be redesigned was the Secretary of State's suite of offices on the seventh floor. But this phase had never been begun because it would have required the incumbent to move to some temporary space elsewhere for a year or more; the prospect of disrupting American diplomacy had stalled the project. I had a different point of view. I came from the construction industry; the banging of hammers and the whine of drills were not noise to me, they were the music of progress. So my staff and I moved to a far corner of the State Department and I called for construction to start. At the end of most days I would relax by going down the corridor to "walk the job."

The result was a heart-lifting space that recalls American history's finest moments and inspires occupants and visitors alike to lift their sights and prove themselves worthy of the setting. Great responsibilities deserve great surroundings, which in turn call forth the best in all of us.

This engaging book by Allan Greenberg carries the meaning of his work on the State Department's great rooms to a wider audience and, for the first time, reveals a truth about our country that our architecture expresses but which we have not fully understood: the fundamental building block of American architecture is the single-family home. Our most successful civic buildings are variations on the basic theme of the citizen's house, and it is through these structures that the idea of a democratic government of the people, by the people, and for the people is made manifest.

In this same spirit, I attended closely to the architectural impact made by our embassy buildings around the world. These embassies have been built in many different styles: some sought to respect the architectural and cultural traditions of the host country; others expressed pride in our history—more than one version of Mount Vernon was erected in a far-off land. In more recent decades we have in some places taken up internationally prestigious building styles, or used the need to construct a new chancery to give an American architect the opportunity to design something wholly innovative.

One thing all our embassies have had in common is the idea exemplified by the Statue of Liberty: openness and welcome. They say to the local population "Come in on your consular or commercial business. Browse our library. Learn about America." Following the rise of terrorism, the bombings of American embassies, and the emergence of weapons of devastating power, however, we had no choice but to "harden" our buildings. Our embassies have come to resemble the fortresses. As you approach, a great jaw of metal yawns at you. You must pass inspection before the jaw drops and you can enter—

only, in some cases, to have to go through other screening devices. The message of our embassies has changed from a welcome sign to "Go Slow; Beware."

We need to ask our architects to work hard to design something better. We need architecture that will say to people that if you come here you will be secure, but you will also be respected and welcome.

Here in this wonderful and insightful book by Allan Greenberg is the spirit that, if captured and built upon, can inspire new architectural designs for this new age of challenge.

INTRODUCTION

FRAGMENT OF AN AUTOBIOGRAPHY

I arrived in the United States at the end of August 1964, accompanied by my wife and two very small children. Standing in the main concourse of the International Terminal at John F. Kennedy Airport in New York, I was aware of being surrounded by voices speaking English with more accents than I had ever imagined existed. An electric energy seemed to pulsate through the ground on which I was standing. At that moment I fell in love with America. It felt as if I had come home.

That passion has intensified during the forty-one years I have lived here. Through hard times I never failed to be touched by the warmth and generosity of Americans from all walks of life. Their kindness invariably shows when one least expects it. I fled from South Africa because of its apartheid system. Like so many who came here from lands beset by oppression, I remain awed by the American political system. An avid reader of American history, I have long regarded the nation's founding documents—the Declaration of Independence, the Constitution, and the Bill of Rights—as miraculous creations, on the order of the tablets of the law God handed Moses. But these remarkable documents were authored by human beings as a part of their revolt against an oppressive colonial master.

One of my great pleasures is to sit in the library at my office and page through the correspondence of George Washington or Thomas Jefferson; to open a biography of James Madison or John Marshall; or to read the speeches of Abraham Lincoln. This may explain why I have one of my offices in Washington, D.C. Sometimes, after dinner at a local restaurant, my wife and I will stroll around the Lincoln Memorial. I choke with emotion every time I read the Gettysburg Address or Lincoln's Second Inaugural. Has any other political leader ever said so much in so few words?[1] At night, the Lincoln Memorial seems to be inhabited by ghosts of Civil War soldiers. I wonder whether they cross the Potomac River from Arlington National Cemetery to mingle with visitors or among themselves. From the interior of the memorial, immured in the presence of the nation's most remarkable president and the Civil War to which he dedicated the last five years of his life, one can see across the reflecting pool to the Washington Monument and the illuminated dome of the Capitol. They stand as a reminder—no, a confrontation—with the nation's founding, with the principles on which it was built, and with the question of what these ideas meant to Washington, to Lincoln, and with what they mean to us now. [Fig. i-1]

At such times it is easy to understand why the Mall is truly the conceptual center of the nation.[2] Because its form embodies the ontological ideals of the Constitution through its relationship with the surrounding civic buildings and city, the Mall teaches us about the ideals in the Constitution and principles of good citizenship.[3] On warm spring days, visitors from every state and many distant nations visit its memorials and museums or picnic under the great sycamore trees. Children are everywhere. On weekends and evenings, locals jog and play softball and volleyball on its lawns near the river. This unusual confluence of the monumental classical setting of domes, porticos, obelisk, and formal rows of trees and the informality of visitor- and family-related activities is a particularly American harmony. I believe George Washington and Pierre Charles L'Enfant, the young French military engineer who served in the

FIG. i-1 *The Mall in Washington, D.C., with the Washington Monument in the foreground and the U. S. Capitol in the background.*

FIG. i-2 *The Bonus Expeditionary Forces camp on the Mall in Washington in 1932 when it was set on fire by the U. S. Army.*

FACING PAGE
FIG. i-3 *The March on Washington on August 28, 1963, to protest racial discrimination viewed from the interior of the Lincoln Memorial. The culmination of this rally was Martin Luther King's "I Have a Dream" speech, delivered from the steps of the Memorial.*

Continental Army and was chosen by President Washington to design the nation's new capital, would be gratified to observe the success of their great enterprise.

The Mall is also the place twentieth-century Americans chose to protest injustice. It was here in 1932 that forty-five thousand unemployed World War I veterans set up a camp—one of many such shantytowns erected nationwide by the unemployed and dispossessed, generally dubbed "Hoovervilles"—to rally in peace for payment of a bonus that had been promised them for their military service. Although the nation was in the middle of the Great Depression, they were forcibly dispersed that July by the U.S. Army, which used bayonets, tanks, and tear gas. Their tents and shacks were then set on fire. [Fig. i-2] The Lincoln Memorial was the location for the groundbreaking concert in 1939 by the great coloratura Marion Anderson, who had been denied the chance to sing at Constitution Hall because she was black.[4] Martin Luther King delivered his historic "I Have a Dream" speech on the steps of the Lincoln Memorial in 1963. [Fig. i-3]

And on a smaller scale, lone protestors and small groups with handwritten placards demonstrate against the scourges of hunger, war, nuclear arms, homelessness, and social injustice on the Mall. In 1996, when the AIDS quilt was spread out there, it extended from the edge of the Capitol grounds to the Washington Monument. The collective creation of thousands of uncele-

brated people, it is one of the most powerful memorials ever designed—and perhaps one that is the most American.[5] [Fig. i-4]

The study of the architecture of my adopted home is a natural extension of my profession and my passionate interest in American history. I came to the United States to study architecture in the master's degree program at Yale. After graduation, I saved for two years to purchase an airline ticket from New Haven, Connecticut, to Charlottesville, Virginia. I thirsted to see the buildings of the extraordinary man who drafted the Declaration of Independence, served as third president, and also excelled as an architect. In 1967 I rented a car at the airport outside Charlottesville and arrived at Monticello about 9:30 a.m. The modest gate was open, so I drove around the hill right up to the side of the house. I wandered around, spellbound, before a gardener found me and explained that the house would not open for hours. I told him my story— about leaving South Africa, living in Europe for three and a half years, studying at Yale, and now, finally, realizing my dream of visiting Jefferson's buildings. He smiled and led me around the house on a tour of the garden and outbuildings, explaining Jefferson's schemes for planting his orchards and vegetable gardens. My guide then opened the front door of the house and invited me to explore the interior at my leisure.

I felt as if I was walking through Jefferson's mind. Experiencing that great house changed my life. It taught me that American architecture was unexpect-

edly different from the architecture of England and the rest of Europe, and from anything I had expected. It was animated by ideas I didn't quite understand, and I looked forward to learning more about them. Later, a docent walked me through every room and supplemented my impressions with details about Jefferson's daily life, his ideas about architecture, and the challenges of preserving the fabric of the house.

Early in the afternoon, armed with directions, I drove into town to see the University of Virginia. Although I was well versed in the history of architecture, able to draw many great buildings to scale from memory, and well acquainted with some of the magnificent buildings in Europe and England, I was entranced by Jefferson's Academical Village. The masterwork of his life, this was surely a creation touched by the finger of God. I wandered around the campus all afternoon and left after 10 p.m. The great buildings of Europe, like Notre Dame cathedral in Paris, seemed to me to be ambassadors from a distant past, whereas Jefferson's university was alive: it embodied a robust and noble vision of a community of scholars living in a democratic society. I imagined living in one of the student rooms and studying under the rotunda of Jefferson's library.[6] In this sleepy town in the Virginia piedmont, the precise confluence of architectural form and meaning captured some quintessential aspect of the spirit of America. It would be true to say that I have spent the rest of my life as an architect grappling with the challenges I confronted that day in Virginia.

In 1968 the nation was convulsed by the escalating war in Vietnam, the political turmoil in the wake of the assassinations of Dr. King and Bobby Kennedy, and the demonstrations that overwhelmed the divisive Democratic National Convention in Chicago. It was also a period of growing concern about "urban unrest"—politicians touted law-and-order platforms in the face of race riots in the inner cities and the growing use of drugs. The previous decade of costly government programs to halt the decline of inner cities had failed. Highways designed to bring suburban shoppers into town instead drew urbanites to new suburban residential developments and shopping centers; the volume of retail sales and manufacturing in urban areas continued to decline, along with center city land values; and the urban poor and working class were stranded by government programs that cleared low-income residential areas and replaced them with middle-income housing.

My background in architecture was very different from that of my American counterparts, most of whom had four-year college degrees prior to entering a graduate program in architecture. I was seventeen years old and just out of high school when I entered a five-and-a-half-year architecture program in South Africa directly out of high school. At a time when architecture schools in Europe and North America were zealously excising study of the past from

FIG. i-5 *The Courtyard of Deanery Garden (1899–1901), architect Edwin Lutyens.*

FIG. i-6 *The Villa Savoye (1928–1931) in Poissy, France, architect Le Corbusier.*

their curricula, our design studios were unusually inclusive. For two-and-a-half years we were taught classical architecture, including many regional variants, and Gothic design. After a year of work experience in an office, we switched to the study of European modernism for two years. Parallel to these design courses were five years of architectural history. Each semester our examinations were five hours long, during which we were required to answer written questions and draw—from memory, to scale, using a T-square and triangle—all the buildings we had cited. By graduation, I had memorized about three hundred buildings. I loved these history courses and the intense immersion in scale, construction technology, symbolism, and language of architectural form they provided.

As a student of architecture at the University of the Witwatersrand, I was attracted to the work of Le Corbusier, the great avant-garde architect in Paris. The dean there, John Fassler, had been part of a coterie of South African architects who aligned themselves with Le Corbusier in the 1920s. I frequently asked Professor Fassler about his memories of that period. We would often move our discussion to the library, where he would open the folio-sized books of the architecture of Sir Edwin Lutyens, the English architect whose work he saw as the most important and exciting. I would open Le Corbusier's *Oeuvre Complète* (the second volume started with a letter from Corbu to his South African admirers and we would animatedly compare their work. [Figs. i-5 & 6] I will always be indebted to this remarkable teacher. Fassler's patience, the clarity of his explanations, and his infinite reserve of tact during discussions with this particularly obnoxious and arrogant student became the model that I used when I went on to teach.

I left school for a year in 1959—my fourth year of study. It was my dream to work for Le Corbusier, so I traveled to Paris armed with a letter of intro-

duction and spent the next ten weeks trying to see him. Between visits to his architectural office at the Rue de Sèvres, I trekked to Poissy to see the Villa Savoye—then a ruin used as a stable by the local municipality, which wished to demolish it—and his other projects in Paris. I was fortunate to meet Pierre Beaudoin, who made Le Corbusier's tapestries, and with his guidance secured other recommendations by showing my somewhat outrageous non-school-related design work. Eventually I was rewarded with an invitation to lunch with the master near his painting studio. The venue was a working-class bar adjacent to a vast railroad marshaling yard. I opened the door and peered through the murky interior, past men in undershirts playing billiards, until I saw Le Corbusier and Pierre seated in a banquette in the far corner. My French was passable, but I was so nervous my tongue seemed glued to my palette. Corbu understood, and I slowly relaxed as he questioned me about the animals and flora of South Africa. The conversation moved on to the peoples of Africa and then India. Architecture was barely broached until the end, when Corbusier talked about his admiration for the design of the new Sydney Opera House by a young and unknown Danish architect, Jørn Utzon. I was profoundly moved when the proprietor refused payment for our meal. It was a privilege, he said, to have Monsieur Le Corbusier at his restaurant.

Corbu then took me to his painting studio. It was on the second floor of an abandoned signal tower that overlooked the railroad tracks and was quite far from his architectural office on the Rue de Sèvres. He patiently commented on my work, showed me some of his new paintings, and then asked what I wanted from him. I inquired about a job in his office. He suggested I return in two or three weeks, as he needed time to consider my request. I met him twice more in his work space—the famous three-meter cube—at the Rue de Sèvres. After initially suggesting a job in the office of a disciple who prepared his construction documents, which I turned down, he offered me a position in his atelier—on condition that I work without pay for a year until I could be "useful." I was crestfallen and explained that I lacked the resources for such an arrangement. Le Corbusier smiled and leaned back slowly. From behind his chair he swung out a large basket, probably Indian, overflowing with discarded and crumpled sheets of tracing paper, and said, "Don't worry! There is nothing you can learn here; there are no rules I can teach you. Remember, no one knows the size of my waste paper basket. Architecture is hard work, a patient search for the right answer." As we shook hands, I was overwhelmed with emotion. I walked down the wide stone stairs of the old convent building in which his architectural office was located and sat on a bench in the Gothic cloister marveling at what had just happened; I also wondered why Europe's cutting-edge architect had located his office in a five-hundred-year-old building.

I spent the remainder of the academic year working and studying in London, then returned to Johannesburg to finish my degree. Soon after, I fled from the racial turmoil in South Africa for life elsewhere. I spent the next year working for Jørn Utzon in Denmark on the amazing Sydney Opera House. I also visited important buildings: Gerrit Rietveld's Schroeder House (1924), the brilliant Sanatorium Zonnestraal (1928) by Duiker and Bijvoet, Alvar Aalto's Neue Vahr apartment building in Bremen (1958–62), Antonio Gaudi's buildings in Barcelona, Le Corbusier's chapel at Ronchamp (1950–54) and his monastery Sainte Marie de la Tourette in Eveux (1956–59). [Fig. i-7] I was amazed by the extraordinary, and as yet unsung, diversity of these twentieth-century buildings. If truth be told, contemporary buildings by Le Corbusier, Mies van der Rohe, Walter Gropius, and Aalto are almost as different from one another as they are from the work of more traditional architects like Lutyens or John Russell Pope.

When Utzon moved his firm to Australia, I spent the next year in architectural offices in Helsinki and immersed myself in the buildings of Aalto. I

FIG. i-8a and b *The Rödabergsområdet housing project (c. 1907) in Stockholm, Sweden, architect Per Olaf Hallman. Drawings by Kerstin Martin and Cecilia Währner.*

then moved to Stockholm for a year to work in the office of Eric and Tore Ahlsen. During that period, I was mystified by the promiscuous destruction of old buildings in Europe and their replacement by undistinguished new ones. Many architects seemed to dislike old sections of cities and looked forward to replacing them with contemporary designs of their own. I wondered if this was really the best approach, aesthetically or socially. I loved exploring the older sections of Stockholm and, on one such ramble, discovered a neighborhood protest against the planned demolition of a working-class housing project. Built under the sponsorship of the Social Democratic party, Rödabergsområdet was a charming complex of yellow stucco buildings arranged around courtyards and connected by archways. It was designed by Per Olaf Hallman in 1907. [Figs. i-8a and 8b] There were flower boxes in many windows, and sheer, white curtains snapped like sails in the breeze. I was enchanted by the architecture and horrified to learn of its proposed demolition. Apparently the laundries, steam baths, and bathrooms were communal and did not conform to current building and health codes.

Although I had trouble understanding some of their accents, residents showed me around the complex; their outrage was palpable. Some invited me into their apartments, where our discussions were well lubricated by cups of coffee and shots of aquavit. I quickly understood that what was occurring was involuntary "replacement;" that is, the complete demolition of a beloved, established working-class neighborhood followed by the construction of new and unfamiliar modern buildings. Such a plan would do a disservice to the inhabitants and their quality of life and destroy the fabric of the city.

After numerous protests, the residents prevailed. The complex was eventually restored and improved by the addition of new bathrooms and kitchens in each apartment. Because the professionals believed they knew what was best for Rödabergsområdet, they hadn't bothered to ask residents what they

FIG. i-7 *The Sanatorium Zonnestraal (1928) in Hilversum, Holland, architects Johannes Duiker and Bernard Bijvoet.*

wanted. Such consultations should have been an essential first step. It all seemed so futile, particularly in the light of the plan for new housing, which would have been a nondescript group of buildings that had no connection to the surrounding architecture or to the lives of Röda Bergen's residents.

My reading around that time added to the ferment I felt. I was thrilled by Jane Jacobs's *The Death and Life of Great American Cities*.[7] More than an eloquent celebration of urban life, it remains one of the most profound indictments of modernistic architecture and city planning ever written. In a bookstore in Stockholm, I happened upon *The Golden City* by Henry Hope Reed, a photographic elegy to lost masterpieces of New York architecture and the mostly mediocre buildings that replaced them.[8] The questions raised in these publications remain pertinent today. Less immediate in its relevance, but more lasting in its import, Vincent Scully's *The Earth, the Temples, and the Gods: Greek Sacred Architecture* introduced a more ecological approach to the relationship of architecture and the landscape by exploring how the ancient Greeks related the architecture of temple complexes to the surrounding landscape they considered sacred.[9] Like Jane Jacobs's approach to urban planning, he raised the level of the debate about the ways in which architecture relates to its surrounding. In April, 1964, the *Architectural Forum* published an astonishing debate between novelist Norman Mailer and Scully in which Mailer asserted that the methodology of modern architects was fascistic—his word for the intellectual arrogance he perceived at modernism's core.

To resolve my intellectual conflict at the time, particularly about the role of architectural history in contemporary architecture and the relationship of new buildings to cities and to the landscape, I began to write about the architecture of Lutyens and Le Corbusier. Because I did not know how to move on in my work as an architect, I also sought an opportunity to study architecture at one of the great universities in the United States. I applied to and was accepted into the master's degree program at Yale, whose chairman, Paul Rudolph, was one of the most dynamic and controversial designers of the time.

Our class comprised twelve students, half of them American and half from abroad. Paul Rudolph was the finest teacher I had ever encountered. Totally committed to architecture, he would often come into our studio at midnight to look at our designs and chat with the two or three students who were there. Although he was considered a ruthless critic, I believe his honesty stemmed from love of architecture and respect for his students. During one such midnight discussion, Professor Rudolph looked at my design for housing based on courtyards, like Röda Bergen, and said, "I bet you've never walked through the courtyards of the Yale College." He drew me a map and said, "Walk through these courtyards on your way home tonight. Look at them again in the morning. They are superb." [Fig. i-9]

I followed the map and was captivated by the intimacy and the charm of the Gothic quadrangles. As I wandered through the courtyards the next morning, my schooling in South Africa became relevant to me. I understood the geometry of the Gothic moldings, the witty use of sculptures, and the picturesque composition of masses, so very different from the ruthlessly balanced geometry of English Gothic colleges at Oxford. Designed by James Gamble

FIG. i-9 *Branford College (1921) at Yale University in New Haven, Connecticut, architect James Gamble Rogers.*

Rogers and John Russell Pope between 1917 and 1940, the courtyards are loved by Yale's undergraduates and alumni and form an important component of the university's identity. Yet in the architecture school, they were despised as detritus from the past.

At this time I also reread the essays on Le Corbusier by the English historian Colin Rowe. "The Mathematics of the Ideal Villa," published in the *Architectural Review* in 1947, was particularly challenging, since it presented the houses of Le Corbusier as a reaction against the legacy of houses by the sixteenth-century Italian architect Andrea Palladio.[10] I also found Luigi Moretti's polemical journal *Spazio*, with his important essays on spatial sequences and on moldings as abstract art.

After graduation from Yale, I was lucky enough to find a job in the city of New Haven's Redevelopment Agency. At the time New Haven was considered the nation's "Model City," and the mayor, Dick Lee, was a national celebrity. As I learned more about the redevelopment program over the next two years, it seemed like a replay of what happened in Rödabergsområdet—except in New Haven, the residents did not prevail. Thousands of homes belonging to poor and working-class families—typically two- or three-story wood frame houses converted to rental apartments—were demolished to accommodate new, low-density middle-income housing developments that lacked any relationship to the surrounding city. This caused great hardship for displaced families. Yet for a fraction of the cost of acquisition and demolition, residents could have been given a combination of grants and loans to repair their houses—and keep their communities intact.

I believed that the city's social fabric and character were being undermined and could not understand why beautiful and urbane older buildings were being demolished to subsidize mediocre speculative development. Even more egregious was a block-wide demolition to make room for a new state highway, Route 34, which bisected the city. The design called for interstate highway standards. The corridor blasted through one side of the central business district, low-income business and residential areas, and a park. Hundreds of families lost their livelihoods and homes. Fifty years later, the grand highway remains unrealized and, for most of its length, the road remains only a little wider than it was in 1940.

That all these situations called for the sacrifice of people's homes—in which they lived, kept their family's possessions, and planned their children's futures—was seldom considered. Dwellings were characterized as "units," abstractions to be tabulated like beads on an abacus. Based upon superficial appraisal, neighborhood businesses were contemptuously referred to as "marginal" enterprises. And when citizens rejected the elitist, sometimes racist, and antiurban dictates of the agency's lawyers, planners, architects, and administrators, the proffered explanation was: you are too ignorant to understand what is best for you. Sadly, most of the politicians who wrote the enabling legislation into law, and professionals who implemented the programs, were white; those affected were poor and mostly black. Redevelopment became a theater of the absurd: the larger the areas of demolition, the larger the federal and state grants and subsidies. Even when smaller budgets and more modest programs

might have better served to improve the life of the community, demolition was the chosen route to ensure a constant flow of federal and state dollars into the city.

Urban renewal in New Haven was a tawdry reflection of Le Corbusier's ideal city: the *Ville Radieuse*. Although Le Corbusier's ideas were compelling for their startling vision and diagrammatic clarity, their influence was an unmitigated disaster for American cities and towns. Given my admiration for his architecture, this lesson came as a bitter blow. Divorced from time and place, his approach to city planning assigned hitherto unimagined authority to architects and planners, most of whom failed to grasp its limitations. No longer confined to a single site hemmed in by adjacent structures; no longer concerned with the integrity of the street or relationships to adjacent buildings, the modern architect was free to ignore the past and jettison any sense of architecture's relationship to society.

As the protests against the war, racism, and urban renewal escalated, I found that the passionate convictions on both sides of the increasing ideological divide were unsettling. All nuanced argument was shouted down. Although the issues were very different, the angry confrontations reminded me of the world I had left behind in Johannesburg. I craved something solid and coherent on which I could focus my attention. I returned to the paper I had started to write in Sweden on Lutyens and Le Corbusier. It became my refuge as the world around me seemed to lose its cohesion. I expanded the paper to include Frank Lloyd Wright. The text, "Lutyens Architecture Restudied," was published in 1969 in *Perspecta #12*, the Yale School of Architecture's influential journal. A revised edition of this text will be published in London in 2006 as a small book, *Lutyens and the Modern Movement*.

In late 1968, the new dean of architecture at Yale, Charles Moore, invited me to join the faculty as a visiting professor. The late 1960s and early 1970s were years of intense questioning rather than rigorous reflection. The sexual revolution and women's liberation movement were also underway. University campuses throbbed with protests against the war in Vietnam, racism, imperialism, military recruitment on campuses, poverty, urban renewal, and a host of other social issues. And the nation's architecture schools were not exempt. At Yale, when I began teaching in 1968, art, drama, and architecture students cornered the university president and provost in the art gallery to protest the paucity of financial aid available to them. At the end of the academic year, the Art & Architecture building burned down under as-yet unexplained circumstances.

In my design studios, I assigned challenging problems involving additions to important old buildings or projects set in historic parts of cities. Because modernist architects believed that most classical and Gothic buildings were simply copied from the past, I created exercises to show students this was false. We made models of unusual and often-overlooked buildings that no longer existed or had never been built—Alvar Aalto's Finnish Pavilion at the New York World's Fair of 1939, sadly demolished, and Hannes Meyer's unrealized Petersschule in Basel of 1926–27. In order to study the work of great architects, teams of two or three students were assigned to design a house as if they were Frank Lloyd Wright. Each year my design studio visited Philip

Johnson at the Glass House in New Canaan. He always showed the students around the estate, diligently answered their questions, and patiently reviewed their designs. Class trips were focused on introducing students to the architecture and urbanism of the nation's past and included visits to historic buildings in Connecticut and walking tours of New York.

I treated my classes as investigations into the nature of different aspects of architecture. No student was ever pressured to follow a particular design approach, and visitors with very different points of view were invited to lecture. But, increasingly under siege from attacks by the full-time faculty in the architecture school, whose views about architecture and education were very different from mine, I decided to resign. I was convinced that the faculty, even though part of a great university, would not enter into a serious dialogue related to the limitations of both modernism and the architectural approach I advocated. This was something I only fully understood the following semester, when I was appointed to the visiting faculty at the Yale Law School. The zeal and confidence with which fundamental questions, often at odds with current legal practice, were debated by law students and faculty had no parallel in any architecture school I had previously visited.

At the time I felt trapped in the middle of a war between modernist architects and the past. I continue to believe there is a better way to resolve the dilemmas on both sides of this divide. I left Yale to focus on developing my office. The challenge I faced in practice was similar to my teaching: is modern architecture intrinsically anti-urban? Could it be expanded to incorporate the despised world of architectural history? Could its elitism be replaced by genuine community involvement? At one point, I stumbled on a concept from Mao (that I believe originated with Einstein): the way one defines a problem limits the nature and range of solutions that one develops. As I struggled to properly define the challenges I faced, I also confronted my first design commission, an addition to the Connecticut State Library and Supreme Court Building (1908–10) by Donn Barber. Influenced by Alvar Aalto, I planned a modern building with large Scandinavian windows with internal blinds and very high insulation properties. [Fig. i-10] In plan, the addition formed a curve connecting Barber's building to a recently completed addition at the rear of the State Library. Instead of Barber's pilasters and attached columns, I indicated a framed steel structure with recessed panels. The rhythm of windows related to Barber's, though the exterior material was limestone rather than more costly granite. I was proud of the design but wondered whether the level of conversation between new and old lacked the intensity found in additions by the great Renaissance masters. For example, I am still awed by Sir Christopher Wren's brilliant Gothic gateway, Tom Tower (1681–82), at Christ College,

FIG. i-11 *Addition to a seventeenth century house in Guilford, Connecticut, designed by the Author.*

Oxford, because it is so obviously new and yet so seamlessly integrated into an older structure. More recently, in the 1930s, James Gamble Rogers created a surprising and restrained Georgian courtyard inside the exuberant Gothic exterior of Davenport College at Yale.

Soon after that first commission, I designed an addition to a beautiful seventeenth-century house in Guilford, Connecticut. [Fig. i-11] Typical of New England, it was prim and taut, covered by wood siding and a steep, shingled roof. The inside of the attic roof was covered with fascinating drawings and notes, a seventeenth-century version of the amazing graffiti artwork that once glorified the dismal world of New York's subway system. I prepared a number of different designs examining how to explore the relationship of the new to the old. I imagined I was using ideas of different architects: Marcel Breuer, Stanford White, and Ithiel Town. The clients' response was instantaneous: they loved the shingle style design. In the manner of a colonial architect, I had simply extended the roof at the rear of the house over a new, asymmetrically placed, one-story addition.

In 1976 I looked back on my twelve years in the United States and tried to assess exactly where I stood. The relationship between new and old at the house in Guilford was, to my eye, more successful than my Supreme Court addition. I also found the process of designing it more exciting because of the necessary historical research into the architectural background of the existing house and the adjacent buildings. Walking around New Haven's ruined redeveloped downtown disheartened me, because I believed architecture was an essential component of urbanism. Like so many foreigners, I was fascinated by New York. But, despite a few important modern buildings, its new architecture was dismal. The mindless agglomeration of new office towers and plazas, like those on Sixth Avenue west of Rockefeller Center, lacked a relationship to each other. Poor architecture and diminished urbanism were eroding the city's essential character. I concluded that, for me at least, modernist architecture lacked an alternative urban vision. I decided to pursue a career as a classical architect. At the time I thought I would just follow this eccentric direction for my own intellectual pleasure. In practice, however, my love affair with American architecture—the work of Thomas Jefferson, H. H. Richardson, Frank Lloyd Wright, McKim, Mead, & White, Arthur Brown, and the countless innovative and daring carpenter-architects of the eighteenth and nineteenth centuries— continues unabated. As I write in 2005, it is particularly gratifying to watch the development of so many young architects who have decided to follow a similar path. The great success of former students and employees in architecture, urbanism, and architectural education is especially gratifying.

A driving force behind my decision was the late Arthur Drexler, the director of the Architecture and Design division of MoMA. Drexler was a modest man; his shy patience hid a restlessly brilliant mind. Largely self-taught in art and architecture, and driven by a commitment to use his position to broaden the debate in architecture, he had shaken New York's architectural establishment with his presentation at MoMA of the work of nineteenth-century students at L'École des Beaux-Arts in Paris between October 1975 and January 1976. The exhibition included their schematic designs, restoration projects, and enormous watercolor presentation drawings, as well as their later architecture. The leading educational institution for architects in the nineteenth century—and the place American architects like Richardson and McKim chose for their training—it was regarded as the bastion of everything wrong with architecture by

BELOW
FIG. i-12 *Proposed Mid-Block Park in Rockefeller Center (1980), New York, designed and drawn by the Author.*

FACING PAGE
FIG. i-13 *Residence (1983-1985) in New Canaan, Connecticut, designed by the Author.*

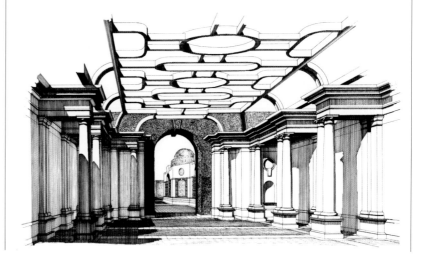

FIG. i-14 *The portico of Gore Hall (1998) at the University of Delaware, Newark, Delaware, designed by the Author.*

FACING PAGE
FIG. i-15 *The Humanities Building (2000) at Rice University in Houston, Texas, designed by the Author.*

modernists. Nonetheless, the exhibition was a huge success and was packed with visitors right up to the last day. Soon after, Arthur asked me to co-curate an exhibition of Lutyens's architecture that opened in 1978 and led to the major Lutyens exhibition in London four years later. I also exhibited a project for a new park in Rockefeller Center and participated in another exhibition, Buildings for Best Products, in 1979. [Fig. i-12] During this period, I designed

the State Courthouse in Manchester, Connecticut, using the shell of an empty supermarket, and was retained to design a number of new houses. [Fig. i-13]

The classical architect's approach to design is very different from that of the modernist. For the latter, the past—everything prior to the advent of modernism in the 1920s—is irrelevant. For a classical architect the past is not dead; rather, it is part of a continuum that includes the present and the unknown future. It is

the same in the practice and study of law. There is no history of the law, for the law is its own living history through the use of precedent, later formalized into the case study method. For both the classical architect and the lawyer, the past is vibrant with precedent and lessons for the present. [Figs. i-14 & 15]

However, not all precedent is equally important. For an architect practicing in the United States, American architecture is basic, as are its roots in the archi-

tecture of England, Holland, Italy, and classical antiquity. This book is an explanation of my quest to understand the architecture of my adopted home and its relationship to the very particular form of democracy shaped by the Constitution and Declaration of Independence. I believe this architecture forms an essential part of the core of this nation. As such, my point of view is iconoclastic. It rejects the common currency that architecture, like painting and sculp-

FIG. i-16 *Proposed Federal Courthouse (1993) in Minneapolis, Minnesota, designed by the Author in association with A. Epstein & Sons.*

ture, is primarily a vehicle for the self-expression of the architect and, as such, is divorced from the daily activities of the people who use the buildings and from the political and social forces that animate the contours of our lives. [Fig. i-16]

Democracy is not something imposed from above. It is more than just a good idea that John Adams and Thomas Jefferson grafted onto colonial life. In the opening paragraph of Democracy in America, Alexis de Tocqueville asserted that democracy is a state of mind that penetrates every aspect of life in this nation. Describing the way one important aspect of democracy, "equality of conditions," is inherent in the nation's life, he writes:

> Soon I recognized that this same fact extends its influence well beyond political mores and laws, and that it gains no less dominion over civil society than over government: it creates opinions, gives birth to sentiments, suggests usages, and modifies everything it does not produce.[11]

The question of the nature of architecture is not the exclusive preserve of the design profession or the academy. It has an impact on the character of our homes, and of the towns, cities, and suburbs in which they are located; the architecture of the schools and colleges to which we send our children; our churches, synagogues, mosques, and other places of worship; our parks and public buildings, and even the debates in the halls of our democracy.

I believe that the endurance of American democracy is the creative masterwork of the American people. The architecture that was created by the same founders who wrote the Declaration of Independence, the Constitution, and the Bill of Rights embodies the ideals of that democracy. And I believe that the American people will always deserve architecture worthy of the noble ideals on which their nation was founded. [Fig. i-17]

FIG. i-17 *Treaty Room (1985–1986) in the U. S. Department of State, Washington, D.C., designed by the Author.*

PREVIOUS PAGES
FIG. 1-1 *Jonathan Mix House (c. 1787–1799), New Haven, Connecticut.*

FIG. 1-2 *A scene from John Ford's masterful The Man Who Shot Liberty Valance (1962). James Stewart is teaching reading and civics to a group of young and old Americans.*

FIG. 1-3 *New Jersey Statehouse (1792) Trenton, New Jersey.*

reat architecture makes great ideas visible. What are the ideas expressed in great American architecture? The answer is simple: American architecture embodies the ideals of democracy for which our revolution was fought and our Constitution created.

What is the significance of this revolutionary idea? A scene in John Ford's masterful 1962 western *The Man Who Shot Liberty Valance* suggests the answer. [Fig. 1-3] In a small frontier settlement, a class of children and adults is learning to read. It is a diverse group, including immigrants from Europe and Mexico and a former slave. Their teacher is a lawyer from the East played by James Stewart. Using the Declaration of Independence as the class text, he asks, "What kind of government do we have?" This is a question many teachers in classrooms throughout the United States ask every day. Nora, a Swedish immigrant, answers that "the United States is a republic and a republic is a state in which the people are the bosses. And that means us."[1]

Nora understands that the American Revolution created a new nation and a new form of government. In order for this endeavor to succeed, the Constitutional Convention intentionally turned upside-down the political ideology of European monarchies, in which the king was the government. Under this arrangement, the monarch is chosen by God and rules by divine right; the people are the king's subjects and have no function other than a source of revenue and service.

King James I of England asserted that his role was to sit "upon GOD'S . . . throne in earth," and that "even by GOD himselfe [kings] are called Gods."[2] [Fig. 1-4] The people were the king's subjects. Louis XIV of France aptly defined this role when he said, "L'Etat, c'est moi"—"I am the state." The U.S. Constitution subverted these claims by defining "We the People" as the gov-

ernment, giving ordinary citizens the responsibility to determine their own destiny as well as that of the nation. The president, the cabinet, and the congress, as well as governors and mayors, became servants of the people. Herman Melville distinguished the status of the citizens of the new nation from that accorded to kings:

> This august dignity I treat of, is not the dignity of kings and robes, but that abounding dignity which has no robed investiture. Thou shalt see it shining in the arm that wields a pick or drives a spike; that democratic dignity which, on all hands, radiates without end from God; Himself! The great God absolute! The center and circumference of all democracy.[3]

As they forged the components of democratic government, the founders also created a new architecture to express their revolutionary vision of society. We see this in two radical aspects of the architecture that developed out of the American Revolution:

First, the basic building block of this new architecture is not the king's palace or the church, as in England and Europe, but is instead the modest single-family house. Because the government is the people, citizens' houses—the homes of members of the government—become the architectural equivalent of the royal palace. [Fig. 1-1] For the first time in history, the ordinary person's house became a work of architecture.

Second, because the idea of the citizen's house is so fundamental to our national identity, to our sense of who we are and how we live, we identify our public buildings by the suffix *house*. Thus, we have state*houses* [Fig. 1-3], court*houses* [Fig. 1-5], fire*houses* [Fig. 1-6], school*houses* [Fig. 1-7], police station

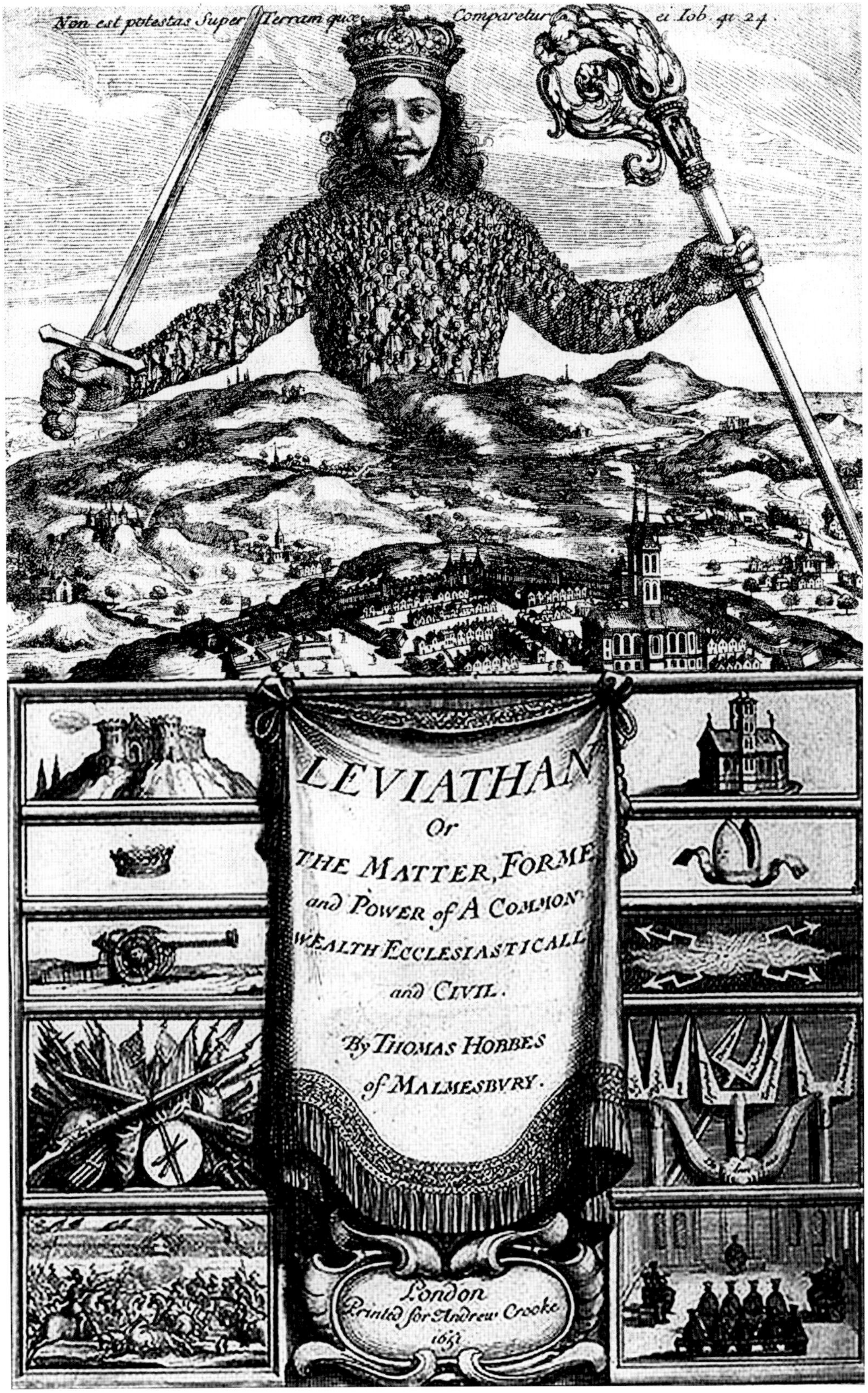

FIG. 1-4 *A detail from the title page of Thomas Hobbes' Leviathan (1651) showing the king's subjects as miniature components of the god-like royal body.*

FIG. 1-5 *Lumpkin County Courthouse (1836), Dahlonega, Georgia.*

FIG. 1-6 *The early twentieth century firehouse of Engine Company No. 1 in Alexandria, Virginia, is an unobtrusive neighbor on its historic residential street.*

FIG. 1-7 *Schoolhouse (1820) in Branford, Connecticut.*

houses, and even jail *houses*. The United States Capitol in Washington, D.C. was originally called the Congress *House*; early city halls in New England and Pennsylvania were town *houses*. The familiar suffix *-house* tells us that a state-*house* is the collective home of all the citizens of that particular state—that is, of the state's government; a court*house* is the home of citizens seeking justice; and school*houses* are the homes of children seeking education.

THE HOUSE AS THE BASIC BUILDING BLOCK OF THE NEW ARCHITECTURE

The basic building block of American governance is the citizen, and the basic unit of American architecture is the citizen's home. It might be difficult today to appreciate how revolutionary it was to assert that an ordinary person's home could be a great work of architecture. Trying to reconcile the provincial modesty of the late colonial and federal house in North America with the obvious grandeur and architectural sophistication of a great English country estate or a European monarch's palace is reasonable in the context of comparing buildings created under royal and democratic governments. A direct comparison of their architectural qualities is taxing because the scope of the aesthetic challenge for each set of buildings is so different. For example, can one credibly compare the modest Mix House [1778] in New Haven, Connecticut, or even the larger and more elegant Octagon House [1800] in Washington, D.C., [Fig. 1-10] with the great entrance wing of Louis XIV's Palais du Louvre [1667] in Paris, or an English estate like Castle Howard (1701–24), or the smaller Coleshill (1658–62). [Figs. 1-8 and 1-9]

In England the country house—both the great estate and the small manor house—served as a seat of local authority. Unlike in France, where the

FIG. 1-8 *The East Façade of the Louvre (1667–1674), Paris, France, designed by Claude Perrault for Louis XIV, and the Octagon House (1798–1800) in Washington, D. C., architect Dr. William Thornton, drawn to the same scale.*

A

B

C

D

FIG. 1-9

A *Castle Howard (1699–1712), Yorkshire, designed by Sir John Vanbrugh*

B *Coleshill (1658–1562), Berkshire, designed by Roger Pratt*

C *the President's House (1732) at the College of William and Mary*

D *townhouse (1720–1750) in Wilmington, Delaware.*

All these buildings are drawn to the same scale as the Louvre and Octagon House.

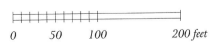

0   50   100   200 feet

FIG. I-10 *The Octagon House (1800) in Washington, D.C., designed by William Thornton.*

FIG. I-11 *The Isaac Potts House (c. 1774) in Valley Forge, Pennsylvania.*

FACING PAGE
FIG. I-12 *The Lady Pepperrell House (1760), Kittery Point, Maine.*

royal palace was the unequivocal seat of power, the kings of England were dependent on both parliament and the landed aristocracy for tax revenues.[4] English architectural historian Mark Girouard writes that "because of their wealth and prestige," owners of country houses "ran the government. . . . The king [though] . . . immensely important . . . [as] the executive head of the government . . . had to rule through someone, and his instruments of rule were the country house owners."[5]

The authority of England's landed aristocracy was expressed architecturally in the size of its houses, the extent of its lands, and the brilliance of the gardens and interiors. In the colonial period in North America, English estates, particularly manor houses, provided a model for the great plantations of Virginia and other colonies. But there are important differences. The American houses have flatter façade articulation, a stiffer appearance, and more austere character. Lacking the bold massing and more muscular architectural detail of many English houses, they demonstrate none of the ease in accommodating houses into the surrounding gardens and landscape.

After the revolution, Americans used the turbulent debates over the drafting of the Constitution and the Bill of Rights to reassess and clarify their relationship to the Old World and its cultural heritage. No longer concerned with imitating English ways, and determined to transcend the limits of their situation on a margin of the civilized world, Americans had the intellectual confidence to jest at the prevailing old-world view that separation from the centers of English and European culture bred inferior people. An ardent commitment to freedom and democracy inspired them to invert the structure of the English and European state and to use the enfranchised citizen as the primary political unit of society, instead of the king.

One result of locating the source of power in the citizenry was that the citizen's house displaced the royal palace and the country house—in both England and colonial Virginia—as the principal expression of governmental authority, and its architecture conveys the special status of the citizen in the new republic. This is why the architecture of federal America embodies a search for building forms that expressed democratic ideals and the aspirations of ordinary people, rather than the tastes of a hereditary aristocracy. Thus the comparison between the Mix and Octagon houses and the palace of a king, or an aristocrat's estate, remains significant despite enormous differences of architectural sophistication, scale, and financial resources. It illustrates the new country's vision of itself as expressed through a set of architectural ideals.

At the time of the American Revolution, most of the aristocracy of Europe and England considered this inversion of values absurd. Most loathed the idea of democracy, and few understood that by the middle of the eighteenth-century, British colonists in North America were already the freest people in the world. Americans had more opportunities to improve their social standing, to own land, and to accumulate wealth than did any group in Europe, even more than the English middle class—despite the benefits accruing from the Glorious Revolution of 1688. Notwithstanding the limited educational and cultural opportunities of frontier life, a spirit of idealism, learning, and innovation permeated revolutionary America. As they constructed their settlements and buildings, Americans looked beyond colonial and English prece-

FIG. 1-13 *The Rev. Henry Whitfield House (1639), Guilford, Connecticut.*

dents to create a more personal architecture. It is not surprising that, led by men like George Washington and Thomas Jefferson, they turned to the rich legacy of classical forms, particularly the architecture of the ancient Roman republic and the independent city-states of the Italian Renaissance.

This process is evident in the evolution of the American house from the early seventeenth century to the establishment of the new nation. The typi-cal colonial house was a simple wood or brick building with a façade that was punctuated by a regular rhythm of windows on either side of a front door. The door was usually the most elaborate feature of the façade. [Fig. 1-12] Some smaller houses had asymmetrical plans or elevations. [Fig. 1-11] Although the first homes the settlers built looked like the houses they had left behind in England [Fig 1-13], the harsh realities of life in the New World

FIG. 1-14 *The Lindens (1754) built in Danvers, Massachusetts, and moved to Washington, D.C., in the 1930s.*

soon compelled them to adapt their designs to local conditions, and their architecture developed strong regional characteristics. New England houses were typically built of wood with thin walls; their embellishments were linear and subtle in character. [Fig. 1-14] Pennsylvania houses were likely to be brick or stone. [Fig. 1-15] The houses of Virginia were often brick and, like those of South Carolina, were characterized by strong, sculptural moldings and deco-

rations. [Fig. 1-16] As the colonists' prosperity and sense of independence increased, their architecture exuded a new optimism that is evident in the simple dignity of even modest farmhouses and vernacular buildings. [Figs. 1-17 and 1-18] The colonial house form continued to be used through-out the nineteenth and twentieth centuries. It remains the quintessential image of the American home. [Fig. 1-19]

FIG. 1-15 *Mount Pleasant (1765), Philadelphia, Pennsylvania.*

FIG. 1-16 *Nathaniel Russell House (1808), Charleston, South Carolina.*

FIG. 1-17 *Octagonal outhouse building at Mount Vernon (c. 1790), Virginia, designed by George Washington.*

FIG. 1-18 *Powder magazine (1715), Williamsburg, Virginia.*

FOLLOWING PAGES
FIG. 1-19 *Beechwoods (1992), Greenwich, Connecticut, designed by the author. The detail is federal, with hyphens and dependencies, is colonial.*

FIG. 1-20
Hammond-Harwood House (started 1774) in Annapolis, Maryland, designed by William Buckland.

FIG. 1-22
The Parthenon (c. 447–432 BC) on the Acropolis in Athens, Greece, as designed by Ictinus.

FIG. 1-21 *Detail of the entrance door at the Hammond-Harwood House.*

FIG. 1-23 *The North Portal of Chartres Cathedral (c. 1194–1220) in France.*

FIG. 1-24 *Grasse Mount (1804), Burlington, Vermont.*

THE TRANSFORMATION OF ARCHITECTURAL SYMBOLS TO REFLECT DEMOCRATIC IDEALS

How did American colonists find ways to make their homes the architectural equivalent of the palace of a European monarch? The most direct way was to modify familiar architectural symbols, even those used to glorify the king, to articulate democratic ideals. An eloquent illustration may be seen at the Hammond-Harwood House [1774–84] in Annapolis, Maryland. [Figs. 1-20 and 1-21] It is a simple brick house with hyphens and dependencies—lower connecting links to wings set on either side of the main house—and its beautiful entrance is the distinguishing feature of the design. It is formed by three familiar components, each of which has symbolic importance: a pediment, the Ionic columns that support it, and the archway that frames the front door. How does this design convey the importance of the citizen's house?

The pediment was used in ancient Greece and Rome to symbolize the dwelling of a god. The Parthenon on the Athenian Acropolis, for example, was the home of Athena, the goddess of wisdom. Doric columns supported its pediment and roof. Because the ancient Greek column is anthropomorphic— a metaphor for a human being—these columns symbolize the citizens of Athens helping to support the roof of the house of their city's patron and protector. [Fig. 1-22] European kings adopted the pediment to articulate the entrance to royal residences and to express the divine right of kings to rule. But set over the front door of a citizen's dwelling in Annapolis, Maryland, the pediment conveys a very different message:

It tells us that here, in the United States, this new democratic republic, the rights and prerogatives that were once reserved for the gods of the ancient world and the kings of Europe now belong to every citizen. Here, through the mecha-

nism of democratic government, citizens determine their own destinies and the destiny of their nation. And they do this without need of a monarch or an aristocracy.

The third symbolic architectural component of the Hammond Harwood House door is an arch. This form was used by the ancient Romans to symbolize the transition between the realms of the living and the dead. Christian churches adapted this symbolism to articulate the transition between the mundane realm of daily life and the church interior, which was considered a portion of the kingdom of heaven on earth. [Fig. 1-23] At the Hammond Harwood House the arch communicates a very different message: It describes the transition between the public sidewalk and the private realm of a citizen's house. *It delineates a privacy that is so sacred that even the United States government may not violate it without a specific and limiting legal authorization.* In this way, Americans adapted and transformed the meaning of accepted architectural symbols to reflect the revolutionary political ideals of their new nation. Forms once used to designate royal authority and religious privilege became symbols of democracy.

THE FEDERAL HOUSE

The use of both pediment and arch is widespread in federal houses. In the early nineteenth century, use of the arch alone became more common. It was used just to articulate the entrance or, in more ambitious designs, as a theme to articulate the overall façade of the house. [Fig. 1-24] In some house designs all three features—pediment, columns, and arch—can be found in an infinite variety of combinations. The details and proportions of new federal features

FIG. 1-25a *The serliana on the side elevation of Mount Vernon.*

FIG. 1-25b *The serliana, or venetian window, from Plate LI in Batty Langley's* The City and Country Builder's and Workman's Treasury of Designs *(London, 1750), which was the source of Washington's design.*

BELOW
FIG. 1-26 *John Pierpont House (1767) New Haven, Connecticut.*

FACING PAGE
FIG. 1-27 *Aerial view of Thomas Jefferson's home, Monticello (1769–1808), in Albemarle County, Virginia.*

tended to be more carefully grounded in Renaissance or ancient Roman models. That was possible in North America, despite its distance from Europe, because many architectural handbooks of measured drawings of ancient Roman, Renaissance, and recent English buildings were published in the late eighteenth century and available in the New World. [Figs. 1-25a and b]

Compared with contemporary English and European buildings, most houses of the colonial, federal, and Greek Revival periods remained provincial in character. The creation of a house and garden that expressed the full measure of the genius of America's founding documents was left to two of our greatest statesmen. The men were also amateur architects, landscape architects, and agronomists: Thomas Jefferson and George Washington.

JEFFERSON AND MONTICELLO

Thomas Jefferson may be the greatest American architect. He despised the colonial buildings of Virginia, finding them to be crude in design in comparison with English and Italian architecture. He set himself the task of revolutionizing American architecture in tandem with the nation's political vision. At Monticello, his farm near Charlottesville, Virginia, he designed and built one of the most intellectually ambitious and beautiful houses in the history of the United States. [Fig. 1-27] Its entrance and garden porticos, dome, orthogonal and octagonal geometry, unusual plan, and beautiful classical interiors present a level of architectural brilliance that continues to hold us in its thrall, even after the passage of two centuries. Rather than adopting colonial precedent by using the pediment and its supporting columns as a broachlike feature on the façade, he integrated them into the roof so that they drive the main axis through the house. By extending the pediment's overscaled Doric entablature completely around the house, he boldly unified the cross-axial composition. [Fig. 1-28] On the garden side, the octagonal dome is the most prominent feature; it is integrated into the mass of the pediment and the angled exterior walls of the formal parlor below it. The composition is framed by raised walkways that connect two small dependencies on either side of the house. [Fig. 1-29]

Most ambitious and unusual is Jefferson's integration of the first- and second-floor windows so that the house appears to be only one story high. The house, in fact, has three stories, for Jefferson carefully hid the attic. [Fig, 1-30] The result is an ambiguity of scale that encourages the perception that this large house is smaller than its actual size. Monticello abounds in other ingenious architectural devices: a master dressing room concealed in unused space above Jefferson's bed, which is also used as a divider to separate his bedroom and study [Fig. 1-31]; a vertical lift hidden in the side of the mantle that brings bottles of wine from the basement cellar to the dining room [Fig. 1-32]; a half-buried transverse service corridor that extends from one side of the house to the other, and a revolving serving door with built-in shelves on one side between the dining room and kitchen service area to increase privacy. [Fig. 1-33]

FIG. 1-28 *Side view of the garden portico at Monticello.*

FIG. 1-30 *Longitudinal section through Monticello showing the relationship between the basement and three-story high interior and one-story high exterior design.*

FACING PAGE

FIG. 1-29 *The raised walkway that extends out from the southeastern piazza on the cross-axis of Monticello. A similar walkway defines the cross-axis on the other side of the house.*

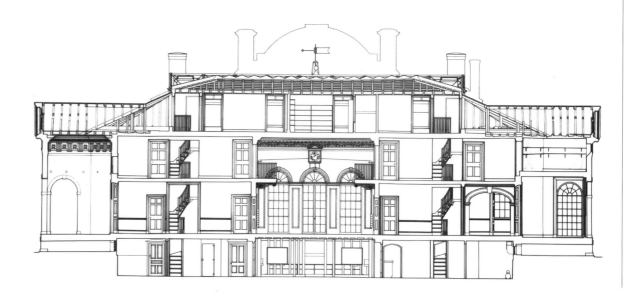

FIG. 1-31 *Jefferson's bedroom with the hidden dressing room in the second floor over the bed.*

FIG. 1-32 *Jefferson's dining room mantle with its hidden dumb waiter, operated by pulleys, to bring wine up from the cellar.*

FIG. 1-33 *Jefferson's serving door with shelves that is located between the dining room and north service passage.*

Monticello is more than just a beautiful building. Walking through its rooms may be likened to entering Jefferson's mind and experiencing the vast range of his intellectual pursuits. Rooms display busts of great men he admired, American Indian artifacts, art, his prized library, and anthropological, botanical, and zoological specimens, some of which were collected by Lewis and Clark during their expedition to the Northwest. [Figs. 1-34] Jefferson also designed many of the furnishings, including clocks, curtains, and a coffee urn. [Fig. 35] Monticello may well be one of the first modern houses in the twentieth-century sense: that is, a house planned as the aesthetic expression of its creator's ideal setting for family life.

Had Jefferson never designed a building, he would have been famous as a scholar, a statesman, author of the Declaration of Independence, and our third president. But our image of him is enhanced because of his architectural genius. His architecture subsumed all the fascinating contradictions of his mind

FIG. 1-34 *The parlor at Monticello with portrait busts of the great men Jefferson admired set between the windows.*

FIG. 1-35 *An obelisk clock at Monticello designed by Jefferson and made by Chantrot in Paris in 1790.*

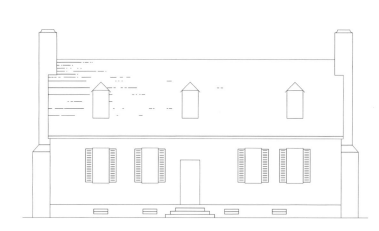

FIG. 1-36a *The first house at Mount Vernon built by Lawrence Washington in 1735.*

FIG. 1-36b *George Washington expanded his late brother's house by adding a second floor in 1759.*

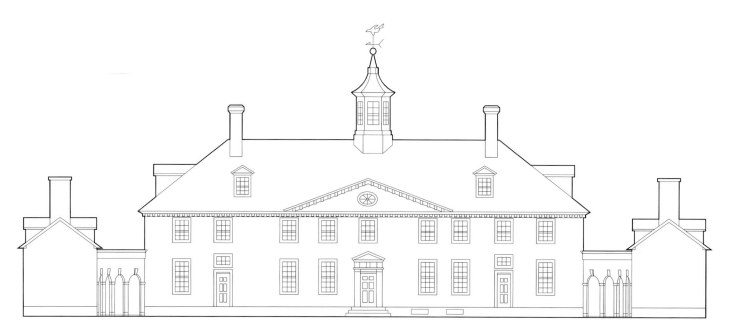

FIG. 1-37 *The final phase of the expansion of Mount Vernon from 1774 through the 1790s.*

and personality and, without turning the pages of history books, we may experience them in the form and furnishings of Monticello.

WASHINGTON AND MOUNT VERNON

George Washington was self-educated; he felt equally at home on the western frontier and in the parlors of Philadelphia. Although he traveled widely throughout the new nation, he never visited England or Europe. He drew his architectural inspiration from books, buildings he visited, and, most important, from his own experience and imagination. Mount Vernon, Washington's estate in Virginia, is important not only because of the inventive planning and dramatic use of asymmetry and informality in the design of the house, but also because it reflects his vision of a working farm planned like a great garden.

The house we see today is an expanded version of an asymmetrical, informal colonial farmhouse that Washington inherited from the estate of his elder

FIG. 1-38 *A downstairs bedroom with a corner fireplace.*

brother, Lawrence, who died in 1752. [Fig. 1-36a] He retained the form and character of Lawrence's house but added another floor in 1757. [Fig. 1-36b] Starting in 1774, he built a large dining room at one end of the house and a master bedroom and study at the other, and then added two open arcades and dependencies. [Fig. 1-37] The additions and arcades on either side are symmetrical and, as a result, frame and even emphasize the asymmetry and informality of the older, center section. At the time, this self-conscious celebration of asymmetry was a radical innovation. On a small farmhouse it would

have been commonplace, but as the focal point of a mansion in the center of a large and very successful complex of five farms, it was unusual.

This informality is carried through to the interior of the house. For example, the fireplaces in the four rooms that open off the center hall are located in corners. A person looking into any of these rooms from the center hall sees the diagonal wall of the fireplace. [Figs. 1-38 and 1-39] This, in turn, deflects the viewer's attention to the interior arrangement of the room. Most corner fireplaces also call for asymmetrical furniture layouts. Washington took the idea of

FIG. 1-39 *The music room with its corner fireplace.*

informality one step further. He planned the house so that doors from one room to another never line up. [Fig. 1-40] This creates a picturesque and relaxed pattern of movement through the house that is very different from the static order of doors lining up one after the other, and of mantles in the middle of walls facing balanced arrangements of furniture. [Fig. 1-41a and b]

Washington's architecture frankly displays its roots in the colonial past alongside its more original features. These include the dramatic, and much imitated, two-story portico he built overlooking the Potomac [Fig. 1-43]; the open

FIG. 1-40 *View from the west parlor at Mount Vernon across the central hall and stair to the dining room.*

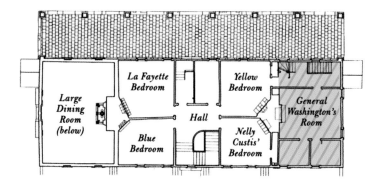

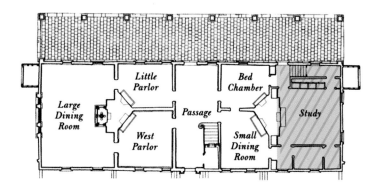

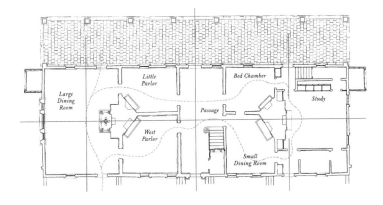

ABOVE AND MIIDDLE **FIGS. 1-41a and b** *The second floor plan of Mount Vernon showing the master bedroom suite planned as a private zone. Washington's study, on the first floor below the master suite, was also planned for privacy.*

BELOW **FIG. 1-42** *The first floor plan of Mount Vernon showing the informal pattern through doors that do not line up with each other.*

hyphens connecting the house to its dependencies; and the planning of the master bedroom and study wing as a private zone to which visitors had no access. [Fig.1-41 and 1-42] The apparent ease with which Washington was able to accommodate the past and the present suggests his confidence as an architect. This approach was very different from Jefferson's, whose desire was to transcend the architecture of Virginia's colonial past and to replace it with strong connections to ancient Rome, to the buildings of Palladio, and in houses, to recent developments in Parisian architecture.

THE FARM AS A GARDEN

The planning of the gardens, farms, and approach road to the mansion house at Mount Vernon also exploits the tension between formal and informal that animates the house's façade and plan. The main axis of the house is projected all the way across the property, from the entrance gate to the estate at one end, through a three-quarter mile long swathe cut out of forests and the center of the house, down to the steep banks of the Potomac on the other. In the 1790s, a visitor approaching the main gate could see the house nearly one mile away at the end of this axis. [Fig. 1-44] But, unlike many on European estates, the axis is not used to approach the house. Rather, Washington directed the road off-axis to one side, and down thirty feet into a dry riverbed that meanders under overhanging forest foliage. [Fig. 1-45] It emerges from the woods climbing up the side of the hill near the house and eventually leads to a pair of white gates on the main axis of the house. [Figs. 1-46 and 1-47] Visitors pass through the gates and enter a walled precinct Washington called the Bowling Green. This is a central lawn framed on either side by trees. In the 1790s, there were also densely planted groves of flowering shrubs through which serpen-

tine roads meandered. [Fig. 1-48] As the visitor moved through these bosques, off-axis, the view of the house was lost. The path eventually arrives at a circular lawn before the front door. The latter reestablishes the main axis that extends through the center hall and down to the river. [Figs. 1-43 and 1-41] At this end of the axis, Washington had to cut another swathe through the tall trees that lined the riverbank in order to secure a view of the Potomac.

On either side of the house at Mount Vernon sit two rows of service buildings that form a striking composition. [Figs. 1-48 and 1-49] In most farms at the time, such buildings were typically located in a more haphazard way. These rows of service buildings are part of a larger composition that includes the cutting garden and conservatory on one side and the vegetable garden and orchards on the other. The character of the composition changes as the visitor moves off axis. [Fig. 1-50] As an important cross-axial element on the main axis from the entrance gate to the river, these buildings and gardens are the core of an even larger composition that includes Washington's five farms.

Each of Washington's farms has a small central group of barns and related buildings that can be seen both from the surrounding roads and

FACING PAGE

FIG. 1-44 *Washington cleared a visual axis from the main gate to the house at Mount Vernon.*

RIGHT

FIG. 1-45 *The road to the house moves off the visual axis and descends into a picturesque dry riverbed.*

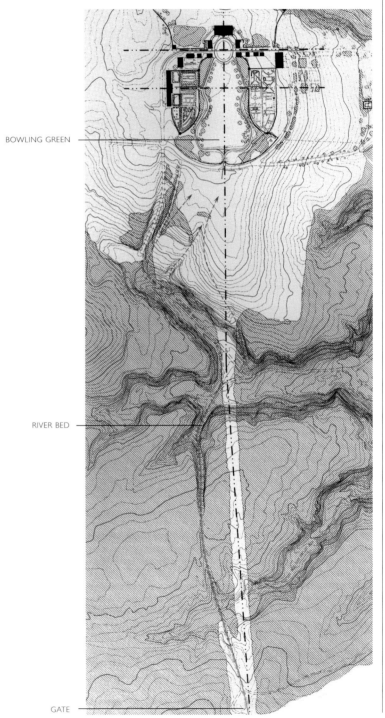

FIG. 1-46 *The first full view of the house as seen from the road through the gates into the bowling green.*

FIG. 1-47 *A plan of the view corridor and road from the front gate to the main house. The precise paths of ascent out of the dry riverbed are not known. Two possible routes are illustrated by the directional arrows.*

BOWLING GREEN

RIVER BED

GATE

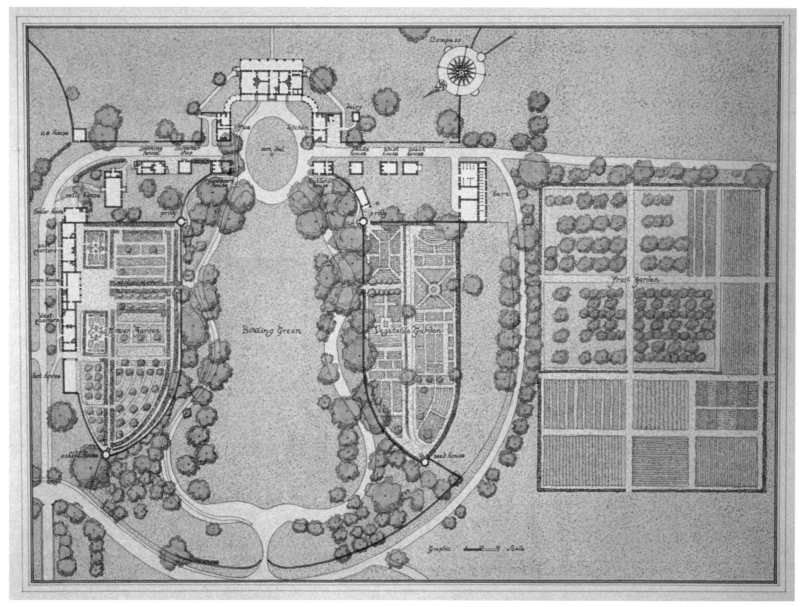

FIG. 1-48 *A plan of the bowling green at Mount Vernon, together with the service buildings and main house in its current state. Sadly, the groves of flowering shrubs on either side of the serpentine roads that Washington planted in the 1780s and 90s no longer exist. The cutting garden, on the left, and vegetable garden on the right, frame the central lawn.*

from within the estate. [Fig. 1-51] For example, the beautiful threshing barn, the center of Dogue Run Farm, is visible from the main road to Alexandria as well as from the road past Union Farm taken by people leaving the main house. [Fig. 1-52] Visitors also have a view of the two-barn complex at Union Farm and the service road that is lined with a double row of trees on each side. The most profound aspect of Washington's design innovations at Mount Vernon is the relationship of the house to its immediate gardens and to the surrounding five farms that comprise the eight-thousand-acre estate. Washington not only planned the house and gardens as a single, integrated work of art but also expanded this idea to include his farms. Relating a house to its pleasure gardens was a common feature of the estates of wealthy citizens of ancient Rome as well as those of Europe's kings and aristocrats. [Fig. 1-53] However, to expand the concept to include all the mundane elements of his working farms—fishery, barns, threshing barn, storage

FIG. 1-49 *View of the north lane with service buildings on either side.*

buildings, roads, fences, forests, and even the river—was something new. It speaks of the ease with which Washington confronted both the man-made and natural worlds, and of the depth of his belief that we should strive to create an ethos of harmonious coexistence between them. Just as the house relates to its garden, so the barns are an integral part of the fields around them. Washington lavishes equal attention and passion on the design of his remarkable threshing barn, his gardens and farms, and his grand dining room. Each one was planned as a significant artifact that is part of a larger work of art, and illustrates Washington's ecological view of their interaction.

Washington and Jefferson were preoccupied with both accommodating the functional details of their houses and celebrating the daily routines of their families' lives. Washington enlarged the scope of this passion to include the design and operation of his farms. This preoccupation with the ordinary facts

FIG. 1-50 *View of the service buildings and main house as seen from the cutting garden.*

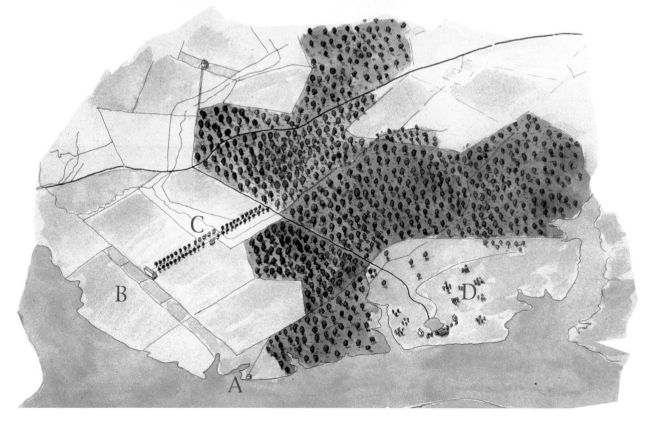

FIG. 1-51 *A conjectural aerial view of Union Farm. Washington planted a double row of trees on either side of the road to the barn complex from the main road. The drawing shows:*

A *the Fishery and Ferry Landing*
B *the Barn complex*
C *roadways*
D *the Main House*

Union Farm no longer exists. The land was sold after Washington's death and developed as housing.

FIG. 1-52 *A re-creation of Washington's remarkable sixteen-sided threshing barn complex. This may be seen today near the main house. In the 1790s it was the center of Dogue Run Farm, which no longer exists.*

and daily routines of life is typical of provincial architecture. In his television series *Civilisation*, the English art historian Kenneth Clark described American federal houses as having "a visionary intensity . . . as they celebrate the world around them."[6] This architecture also demonstrates a lack of interest in questions related to the appropriate refinements of established architectural styles. For Clark they possess a "simple, homespun, independent air," an "almost rustic classicism that stretches right up the Eastern seaboard of America . . . producing a civilized, domestic architecture equal to any in the world."[7]

Washington's approach to architecture was very pragmatic. Passionately focused on the success of the new nation's experiment in democratic government, he regarded ideology as a distraction that could prove fatal to a field commander or to the nation's first president. This held true even in architecture. Washington was not interested in Jefferson's desire to excise the nation's English architectural roots. He had more sympathy with Jefferson's search for architectural roots that extended further back in time to the ancient Roman republic. Although theoretical speculation on such questions bored him, he concurred with Jefferson's belief that architecture should be the preeminent embodiment of the new nation's values. Both men celebrated the daily routines of family life and of farm management through their architecture. Monticello and Mount Vernon stand as statements of the new nation's ideals and aspirations.

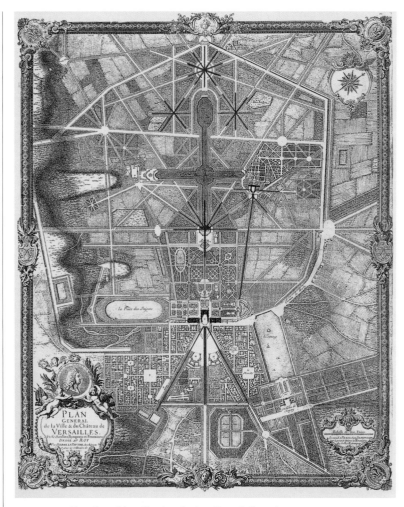

FIG. 1-54a *The plan of Versailles described on Pierre LePautre's "Nouveau Plan des Villes, Château, et Jardins de Versailles," (1710).*

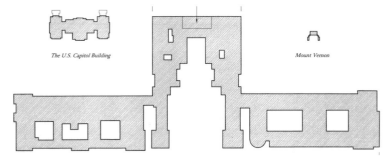

The U.S. Capitol Building

Mount Vernon

FIG. 1-54b *The massing of the palace of Versailles and the house at Mount Vernon drawn to the same scale.*

FACING PAGE

FIG. 1-55 *The Royal Walk and its gardens and fountains at Versailles. The foreground sculpture is the Apollo fountain (1668–1671) by Jean-Baptiste Tuby.*

FIG. 1-56 *The forecourt of Versailles showing the brick and masonry walls of Louis XIII's original château.*

A useful way to illustrate some differences in the significance of architecture in a democracy and under a monarchy is by contrasting the creative endeavors of two men who were crucial figures in the history of their respective nations. Washington transformed a working farm into a work of art at Mount Vernon, and Louis XIV created the palace and gardens at Versailles. [Figs. 1-54a and b] The palace at Versailles and its surrounding pleasure gardens, forests, and hunting preserves were planned with multiple axes and cross-axes that lured the eye with seemingly endless vistas in all directions. The elaborate composition and sheer magnificence of the vast network of gardens at Versailles were planned with an architectonic clarity that aptly described the all-encompassing jurisdiction of the sun-king. [Fig. 1-55] The farms that supported the thousands of retainers, ministers, resident aristocrats, and servants are either not on the plans or are located some distance from the palace and its grounds. Seemingly all of France was the farm that supported the magnificence of the sun-king's life and surroundings.

But Versailles was more than its aesthetic planning; it was primarily an exercise in power, a way for the king to control the French nobility. Living at Versailles kept as many as ten thousand aristocrats away from their estates, away from the primary source of their economic and political power, and isolated from the political aspirations of the middle classes. Their lives were an endless pursuit of pleasure—except that the point of their existence at Versailles, the real work, was pleasuring the king. But the loans that were necessary to maintain this pursuit of pleasure and their place in society were now dependent on the king's generosity. Louis's munificence also extended to the merchants, workers, and peasants who were dependent on his public works projects, his programs to encourage industry and agricultural production, and his reform of France's administrative, tax, and judicial systems. Under Louis XIV, every person depended on the king in the same way that the natural world derived sustenance from the sun.

In comparison to Louis's cunning use of architecture as a tool of statecraft, Washington's modest experiments in agronomy, architecture, and gardening seem simple. Lacking an overt political purpose, his goal was to improve farm productivity, to enhance the lives of his family, and to explore the aesthetic ramifications of his ideas and political convictions. Yet these estates share three characteristics. First, the original house on each property was retained as the core of everything that was created around it. [Figs. 1-36 and 1-56] Louis refused to replace his father's hunting lodge of 1631–34 just as Washington kept his brother's house. Second, they depended on a significant underclass of servants. In the United States, this underclass comprised African slaves. Alone among the nation's founders from Virginia, Washington struggled with this blight on American history. Although he sought a way to free his slaves without initiating the separation of the southern states, he was only willing to do so upon his death. Third, both estates were residences that served broad political functions. During the seventeen years between Washington's victory at Yorktown and his death in 1799, Mount Vernon was the unofficial "White House." For many important visitors, the pilgrimage to Virginia to pay their respects to the new nation's president was almost as essential as the trip to Versailles to the courts of Louis XIV, Louis XV, or Louis XVI.

FIG. 1-57 *Tudor Place (1805–1815), Washington, D.C., designed by William Thornton.*

FIG. 1-58 *Hope Plantation (1803), Windsor, North Carolina.*

THE HOUSE AS AN EXPRESSION OF DIFFUSE POLITICAL POWER

Today, democracy in the United States is so firmly established that we often forget that the outcomes of the Revolutionary War and of the Constitutional Convention were far from certain. It seemed improbable, if not impossible, that a sparsely populated group of colonies with their citizen soldiers could defeat the most powerful professional army in the world. It was even more improbable that they would then be able to unite and create a new political system predicated on the belief that power need not be concentrated in the hands of a king but could be shared between branches of government "among states within a state and that the sharing of power and the balancing of forces can create not anarchy but freedom."[8] Historian Bernard Bailyn tells us that the ambitious scope of this enterprise increased the likelihood of failure. American revolutionaries were warned of the "inevitability" of a descent into "conflict and into chaos" and "of the folly of defying received traditions."[9] How could they, an "obscure people" isolated by an ocean from European civilization and precariously placed at the edge of the wilderness, know more than "the established authorities that ruled them and had governed their forefathers for centuries? How could they create something freer, ultimately more enduring than what was then known in the great centers of European and English culture and learning?" Most revolutionary-era Americans understood the tenuousness of their experiment in self-government. That may explain why they devoted so much effort and so many resources to creating a new architecture to celebrate and reinforce their democratic ideals.

These democratic ideals continue to serve us well. They provide the core of our identity as Americans and remain the quintessential underpinnings of American architecture. This is why the homes and public buildings of late colonial and federal America that they inspired remain distinctly modern, and why Americans have never stopped creating them anew. It is why we continue to design and build such houses today. Their extraordinary variety speaks of the passion, ingenuity, and inventiveness of their architects, builders, and owners. [Figs. 1-57 and 1-58] These houses are so profoundly associated with the inception and maturation of the nation that they accord with our deepest notions of what an American home should be like. That is why all the design preoccupations of the nineteenth and early twentieth centuries, including Greek and Colonial Revival, the arts and crafts movement, and the shingle style have been incorporated into the ever-expanding canon of American colonial and federal architecture, right up to the present. [Figs. 1.59 and 1.60] In addition, it is why citizens are free to explore and pursue more personal, often idiosyncratic, forms in the architecture of their own homes. It may explain why Frank Lloyd Wright, one of America's most original and influential architects, formulated his style designing houses.

The history of American architecture, unlike that of centuries before it, is not written as a great symphonic expression of power in cathedrals and palaces, of God and God's kings on earth. Rather it is a song composed of small houses that may be seen as the expression of diffused power, of the dignity and the authority of the American citizen in a republic. It is in this sense that the citizen's house is indeed the equivalent of a royal palace. This equivalence became possible because the founders took the radical step of trusting the people and giving the citizens a philosophical vocabulary and political language with which to pursue their own destinies, as well as that of the nation and its architecture.

FIG. 1-59 *Isaac Bell House (1883) in Newport, Rhode Island, designed by McKim, Mead, & White.*

FIG. 1-60 *Residence (1997) in Washington, D. C., designed by the Author.*

PREVIOUS PAGES
FIG. 2-1 *Maryland Statehouse (1772–1787), Annapolis, Maryland.*

FIG. 2-2 *Courthouse (1729), Plymouth, Massachusetts.*

FIG. 2-3 *Townhouse (1727), Marblehead, Massachusetts.*

The people reign over the American political world as God rules over the universe.[1] — ALEXIS DE TOCQUEVILLE

The founders of the United States created a nation with a new form of government, one that embraced the proposition that the source of authority is the citizenry, not the monarchy. They also offered a philosophically parallel set of architectural ideals. Because "We, the People" constituted the government, the citizen's house became the equivalent of the king's palace, which made the private house our primary symbolic expression of civic architecture.

That led to a second, equally radical idea: affixing the suffix *-house* to public buildings, which suggests that our public buildings serve as the government's—that is the citizens'—symbolic home. Thus, we have state*houses* [Fig 2-1], court*houses* [Fig. 2-2], fire*houses*, school*houses*, police station *houses*, and even jail *houses*. Early city halls were called town *houses* or, literally, the *house* that belongs to the citizens of the town. [Fig. 2-3] The Congress *House* and the President's *House* were the original names George Washington chose for the United States Capitol and the White House in Washington, D.C. That is why the architectural history of our public buildings is rooted in the nation's evolving concept of the ideal house. From colonial times to the mid-twentieth century, three different house models have animated this architecture, both as form and symbol: the colonial house, the ancient Roman and Greek temple, and the U.S. Congress House or, as it was later renamed by President Jefferson, the Capitol.

THE COLONIAL HOUSE AS A MODEL FOR PUBLIC BUILDINGS BEFORE THE REVOLUTION

The idea of the citizen's home serving as the basis for the design of public buildings is, in large part, a legacy of the Puritan settlers. In England, Puritans were compelled to worship secretly; they usually did so in houses or barns. Because of that practice, they arrived in New England without any architectural precedents for planning their houses of worship. Faced with this challenge, they invented a new type of building, the meeting*house*—literally, a house in which to meet. [Figs. 2-4] It specifically evoked the image of a home, a place where the larger family of local Puritans could gather for prayer and fellowship.

The earliest New England meetinghouses were square, one-room buildings covered by a simple hipped roof (a roof with all sloping sides). Some had a small gable or a dormer window above the entrance doors. Lanterns were sometimes placed over the center of the roof. These buildings were a generic reiteration of the early New England house, albeit transformed into a single, very large room defined by four walls. By the late seventeenth century, meetinghouses tended to be rectangular and more literally houselike in appearance.[2] [Fig. 2-5]

American Puritans thus translated the memory of secret meetings in the homes of their fellows into a distinctive architectural form. The idea of meeting in a house, and the even more remarkable idea of using the suffix *-house* to designate public buildings, may have been supported by other sources. An

CLOCKWISE FROM TOP LEFT
FIG. 2-4 *Old Ship Meetinghouse (1681),
Hingham, Massachusetts.*

FIG. 2-6 *First Church of Christ (1814), New
Haven, Connecticut, designed by Town and Davis.*

FIG. 2-5 *Hans Herr Mennonite Meetinghouse
(1719), Lancaster, Pennsylvania.*

FIG. 2-7a *First Townhouse (1658), Boston, Massachusetts.*

FIG. 2-7b *Second Townhouse (1713), Boston, Massachusetts. After the Revolution it served as the Commonwealth's statehouse until construction of the new statehouse in 1795.*

FACING PAGE

FIG. 2-8 *Chowan County Courthouse (1767), Edenton, North Carolina.*

obvious one may be the British House of Commons, or colonial Virginia's legislature, the House of Burgesses—literally, the House of Citizens. It is also possible that the seventeenth-century Puritans, many of whom were able to read Hebrew, knew that in the Bible the word *beit*, or house, is used to designate the temple in Jerusalem, the house of God.[3] The same word was also used to designate community buildings, such as the *beit din*, house of judgment or court*house*, and *beit ha midrash*, house of study or schoolhouse.[4]

The colonial meetinghouse was used for religious activity as well as for civic functions such as town meetings, court sessions, and other community gatherings. This unusual practice was rooted in the Puritans' rejection of the ideal of consecration—of human beings, buildings, or wafers and wine. They believed that "no place is capable of any holiness, under pretense of whatsoever dedication or consecration."[5] Refusing to recognize a distinction between religious and secular life, Puritans posited a "priesthood of all believers." What counted was the "spirit in which one did the work of every day; not the kind of work it was, but how one did it."[6] During the seventeenth century, the meetinghouse was the center of the community's spiritual and secular life. For the early Puritans, the church was "the body of believers . . . not the visible [architectural] structure."[7] That is why other functions—town government, court trials, and school—were allowed to take place in the meetinghouse. This all-embracing view of religious life was based on the belief that there was "no place which render(ed) the worship of God more acceptable for its being there performed."[8]

This changed in the eighteenth century. In 1723 Puritans in Norwalk, Connecticut, decided that the only activity that would be permitted in their meetinghouse would be "what is consistent with . . . the pure and special serv-

ice of God." They also initiated a movement to construct separate buildings—courthouse, town house, and schoolhouse—to provide for the community's legal, political, and educational needs.[9] [Fig. 2-6]

THE COLONIAL TOWN HOUSE, COURTHOUSE, AND JAIL HOUSE

The American colonies were governed by the crown in London. The king appointed governors; elected legislatures, such as Virginia's House of Burgesses, were advisory. For that reason, there was only a very limited tradition of planning buildings to house democratically elected representatives. It was only at the local level, where the citizenry enjoyed more autonomy, that more relevant architectural traditions were established.

The early New England city hall, or town house, became the venue for town meetings. There, citizens governed themselves by voting on important issues. The town house was thought of as the house belonging to all the citizens of the town. At Northampton, Massachusetts, for example, the old Meeting House was affectionately known as "our town's house."[10] The town house could also serve as a court of justice, a venue for merchants to meet, and sometimes even a schoolroom.[11] The first town houses looked like sixteenth-century English buildings. [Fig. 2-7a] They were often located in the middle of the road and had open ground floors to accommodate covered markets for transactions related to commercial instruments like promissory notes and bonds.[12] But very soon new town houses were built to look like very large homes—and took on a distinctly American cast. [Fig. 2-7b]

FIG. 2-9 *Bellair Plantation (1734), New Bern, North Carolina.*

FIG. 2-10 *Northampton County Courthouse (1730), Northampton, Virginia.*

FACING PAGE CLOCKWISE FROM TOP
FIG. 2-11 *King William Courthouse (1710), King William County, Virginia.*

FIG. 2-12 *Old Stone Jail (1828), Palmyra, Virginia. The building, designed by General John Hartwell Cocke, shows the colonial practice of building house-like jails continued into the early nineteenth century.*

FIG. 2-13 *Old York County Gaol (1653), York Village, Maine.*

The third important colonial public building was the courthouse. Not surprisingly, the early colonial courthouse was also inspired by local domestic architecture and was also simple in mass and austere in design. [Figs. 2-8 and 2-9] In Virginia, the first courthouses were built of wood and described as "hardly distinguishable from dwelling houses."[13] [Fig. 2-10] But this was not the only model for Virginia's courthouses. The more typical eighteenth-century courthouse was a one-story brick building with a T-shaped or rectangular plan. It had the scale and appearance of a single-story local house on three sides, but the front façade was an open arcaded porch—a feature unique to courthouses in colonial Virginia.[14] [Fig. 2-11] The porch provided shelter from the weather and served as a gathering place for citizens. This was a particularly important amenity because most colonial courthouses lacked an entrance vestibule: the front door opened directly into the courtroom.

The local jail house was usually built near the courthouse. The first jails were simple additions to the jailers' homes. At the York County Gaol (1653) in York Village, Maine, both the holding cells and the courtroom were part of the jailer's home. [Figs. 2-12 and 2-13] In colonial Virginia, the Act of 1647 mandated prisons be "such houses provided for that purpose" or be "built according to the ordinary forme of Virginia houses."[15]

The colonial schoolhouse was a small, houselike building. [Fig. 2-14] Education in the colonies depended on a disjointed collection of local schools. The extent and effectiveness of schooling depended on each community's commitment to education. In 1647, Massachusetts enacted the first statute in British North America to create a school system. These schools were to teach students the "ability to read and understand the principles of religion and the capital laws of the country." In New England, meetinghouses also served as classrooms.

FIG. 2-14 *Nathan Hale Schoolhouse (1750), East Haddam, Connecticut.*

FIG. 2-15 *The Old College (1638) at Harvard in Cambridge, Massachusetts.*

FIG. 2-16 *Stoughton Hall (1699), center, at Harvard College, Cambridge, Massachusetts.*

Whenever a new meetinghouse was built, the old one was then usually used as a school and town house. There were also "dame schools" operated by a widow or unmarried woman who used part of her home as a classroom.

The Puritans were particularly concerned about education. In 1636, only sixteen years after landing at Plymouth Rock, they founded Harvard University. Its first building, the Old College (ca. 1644), also known as Harvard Hall I, looked like an English Tudor house with an E-shaped plan and gabled roof. [Fig. 2-15] Built soon after, Stoughton Hall I (1699) was described as "one house multiplied by three."[16] [Fig. 2-16]

FIG. 2-17 *Statehouse at Annapolis, drawn by G. W. Smith in 1810.*

FIG. 2-18 *Upton Scott House (1762–1763), Annapolis, Maryland.*

FIG. 2-19 *Ohio Statehouse (1803), Chillicothe, Ohio.*

THE HOUSE PARADIGM AFTER THE REVOLUTION

The use of the house as a symbolic architectural model for public buildings continued after the revolution. Like the meetinghouse, the statehouse was a new American building type. Statehouses contained chambers for the upper and lower legislative houses, offices for the governor, and the state's Supreme Court. The Maryland Statehouse (ca. 1772) in Annapolis was one of the first built after the defeat of the British. [Fig. 2-17] It is a symmetrical building with large, double-hung windows, a houselike porch at the entrance, and a tall, recklessly bold lantern that beckons citizens to come to participate in the deliberations that will determine the future of the state. A roof pediment marks the entrance to the building and enunciates the same political symbolism as the entrance door of the nearby Upton Scott House (1762). [Fig. 2-18] The statehouse is the culmination of the tradition of planning public buildings as large versions of local houses. Although it was eventually supplanted, the house model for statehouses remained popular in frontier states because it was easy to design and to build. [Fig. 2-19]

FIG. 2-20 *Schoolhouse (1894), Stone Lagoon, California.*

FIG. 2-21 *A class photo if front of a sod schoolhouse (c. 1908), Decatur County, Kansas.*

FACING PAGE CLOCKWISE FROM TOP
FIG. 2-22 *The Russell County Courthouse (1799), Dickensonville, Virginia. The courthouse is the smaller building on the right. When it was no longer used as a courthouse, the building served as a farmhouse and the L-shaped wing was added.*

FIG. 2-23 *New London County Courthouse (1784), New London, Connecticut.*

FIG. 2-24 *Townhouse (1771), Windham, Connecticut*

SCHOOLHOUSES, COURTHOUSES AND TOWN HOUSES AFTER THE REVOLUTION

From the seventeenth century until World War II, schools in rural communities were typically one-room, houselike buildings made of local materials including clapboard, shingles, logs, and sod. [Figs. 2-20 and 2-21] In 1913, 50 percent of all children in the United States were enrolled in 212,000 such schoolhouses. In 1984, 85,000 of these schools were still in use as schools. Familiar and unpretentious, these public schools also transformed children into informed citizens who, upon reaching majority, would be capable of taking part in the exercise of government. For new settlers and their children, attending free public school was an opportunity to study English and learn about the responsibilities of citizenship in their new homeland.

The courthouse and town house also continued to develop the house paradigm. [Figs. 2-22 and 2-23] The courthouse in New London, Connecticut (1784), is an ambitious version of a local house. [Fig. 2-24] It has a bold, three-tiered entrance with rustication around the door, a *serliana* window (a design motif from the Italian Renaissance with a center arched window and two smaller rectangular windows on either side) on the second floor, and a small roof pediment that caps the composition. These features illustrate the architect's search for ways to retain the symbolism of the house while also moving beyond the limitations of colonial design. Virginia's arcaded colonial courthouse also served as a model but usually took the form of a two-story building. [Fig. 2-25] The colonial house model was replaced by federal and then Greek Revival styles. [Fig. 2-26] Houselike court buildings continued to be constructed in the South, the Midwest, and California throughout the nineteenth and early twentieth centuries. [Fig. 2-27]

The significance of these house-inspired public buildings is apparent when we compare an American courthouse with the European *Palais de Justice*. The designation **palace** reflects the divine majesty of the monarch and a venue where the king's justice is administered. The architectural forms and masses of these buildings tend to dominate, even overwhelm, their surroundings. [Fig. 2-28] That approach to the design of public buildings stands in sharp contrast to the American house-based model, which strove to create a new civic architecture, one in which a citizen is at ease and feels a sense of ownership, one in which democratic ideals are manifest.

The full flowering of this symbolically potent approach to public architecture was undermined by Thomas Jefferson, who presented the new nation with a very different, but equally compelling, vision.

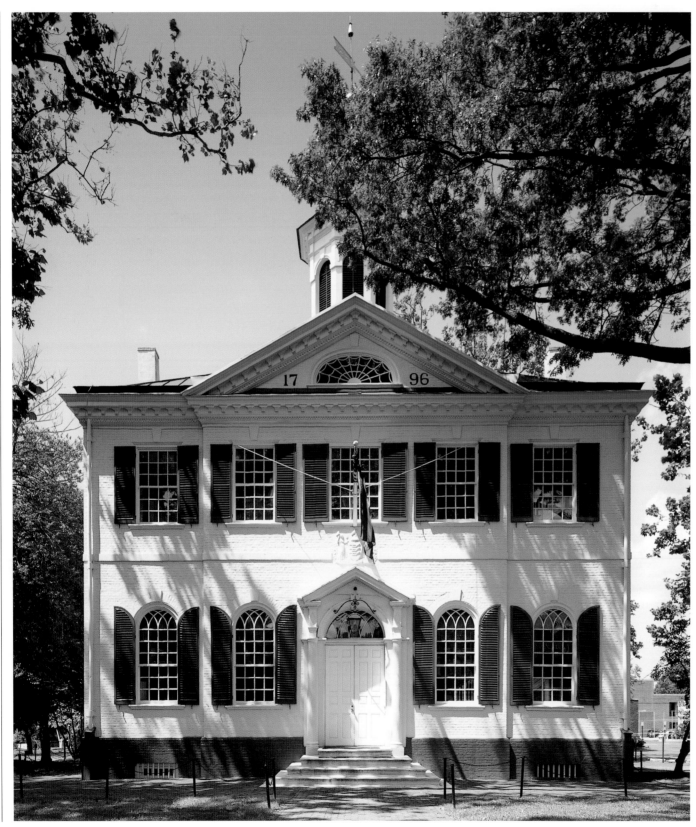

FIG. 2-26 *Burlington County Courthouse (1796), Mount Holly, New Jersey.*

FIG. 2-25 *Caroline County Courthouse (1830), Bowling Green, Virginia.*

FIG. 2-27 *Courthouse (1901), Eagle, Alaska.*

FIG. 2-28 *Palais de Justice (1866-1883), Brussels, Belgium, designed by Joseph Poelaert.*

FIG. 2-29 *Engraving by W. Goodacre (1831) of the Virginia Capitol designed by Thomas Jefferson. The main stair in the front of the building was constructed later.*

FIG. 2-30 *Maison Carrée (20 BC), Nîmes, France.*

FACING PAGE
FIG. 2-31 *Virginia Capitol (1701–1705), Williamsburg, Virginia.*

FIG. 2-32 *Sir Christopher Wren Building (1695–1699), College of William and Mary, Williamsburg, Virginia.*

THE CLASSICAL TEMPLE
AS A MODEL FOR PUBLIC BUILDINGS

In 1785, when he was serving as America's minister in Paris, Jefferson was asked by the Virginia General Assembly for advice on the design of a proposed Virginia capitol—as the statehouse was called—to be built in the new capital city of Richmond. [Fig. 2-29] Working with the French architect Charles-Louis Clérisseau, Jefferson created a revolutionary design that established a major shift in direction and a more ambitious standard for the new nation's public buildings.

It was inspired by an ancient Roman temple, the Maison Carrée (42 B.C.) in the southern French city of Nîmes. [Fig. 2-30] In a letter to James Madison, Jefferson described this temple as "one of the most beautiful, if not the most beautiful and precious morsels of architecture left us by antiquity."[17] Writing to Maria Cosway, a friend in Paris, he described "gazing whole hours at the Maison Quarrée, like a lover at his mistress" and being "nourished with the remains of Roman grandeur."[18] Why did Jefferson propose a Roman temple, the house of a god of the ancient world, as a new model for Virginia's legislative building? Why did he believe that "the noble architecture of antiquity [is] the constant measure of permanent values"?

First, he wanted to develop a stronger association between the classical temple—the house of Greek and Roman gods, whose prerogative it was to determine the destiny of individuals and nations—and the "home" of the government, the people of Virginia. Although his symbolic references were more ambitious, Jefferson's design was, in part, a further development of the

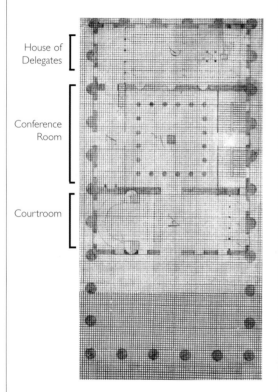

House of
Delegates

Conference
Room

Courtroom

FIG. 2-33 *Plan by Jefferson (1785) for the Virginia Capitol, Richmond, Virginia.*

RIGHT
FIG. 2-34 *Conference room in the Capitol in Richmond. The statue of Washington by Jean-Antoine Houdon, commissioned by the State of Virginia in 1784, still occupies the center of the room.*

FACING PAGE
FIG. 2-35 *The Old House Chamber and its public gallery in the Capitol at Richmond.*

FIG. 2-36 *View of Richmond painted by Benjamin Henry Latrobe in 1798.*

Puritans' idea of a house as a metaphor in the architecture of public buildings. Second, Jefferson believed that the Maison Carrée was built during the period when ancient Rome was a republic; he wished to associate the new nation's republican form of government with that of ancient Rome.[19] In doing so he was building on the earlier legacy of Governor Francis Nicholson, who had planned Virginia's previous capital city of Williamsburg in 1699. Nicholson was the first to name the building that housed the legislative body and royal governor's office "the capitol."[20] [Fig 2-31] Finally, he associated the temple, as well as other religious buildings, with the principles of "trust and inviolability."[21]

Jefferson also felt contempt for much of Virginia's colonial architecture. He described many of the wood houses in the state as "ugly and uncomfortable;" the College of William and Mary and the hospital at Williamsburg as "rude mis-shapen piles, which, but that they have roofs would be taken for brick kilns;" and the state's third capitol as only "tolerably just in its proportions and ornaments."[22] [Fig. 2-32] This dissatisfaction also fueled his drive to chart a new direction for Virginia's public buildings.

Jefferson's design for the new capitol shows a templelike building with an unusually large portico. This feature is an architectural invitation to the state's citizens to enter and participate in their state government.[23] It is a more monumental version of the domestic entrance porch of the Maryland Statehouse. Like the arcades of the state's older colonial courthouses, it is a gesture of inclusion that also promises shelter from the elements. [Fig. 2-33] The plan of the capitol balances the accommodations for the judicial branch in the front of the building with that for the legislature in the rear. Between them, in the center, is a great two-story public space covered by a dome. [Fig. 2-34] Designated the "Conference Room," it fulfills the Virginia constitution's call for such a room to be used during elections for depositing and examining election ballots for each house and the governor. The room can be entered directly from the outside by small staircases on either side of the building. At the time of its completion, the conference room was the most spectacular interior space in the new nation. It served as a fitting setting for Jean-Antoine Houdon's great sculpture of Washington as a citizen-soldier that still occupies the center of the room. Unlike the Maryland Statehouse, where the dome is prominently featured on the exterior, the Conference Room dome is completely contained within the roof. Jefferson did not want to distort the Roman temple form by expressing it on the exterior. He located the upper house chamber on the second floor above the courtroom.[24] As at Annapolis, there are provisions for spectators' galleries in both the upper and lower houses.[25] [Fig. 2-35]

The most dramatic feature of the building may be its setting high on a bluff overlooking the James River. A white temple proudly marking the political center of Virginia's fledgling capital, it was the largest and most prominent building in Richmond at the time. [Fig. 2-36] Gathered around its skirt were the town's mostly small, wood buildings. In 1791 William Loughton Smith, a visitor from South Carolina, described the "immense capitol towering above the town on a lofty eminence . . . [as] the first thing which strikes the traveler."[26] One hundred and fifty years later, architectural historian Fiske Kimball described it as "a frontispiece to all Virginia."[27]

Jefferson found the formal simplicity and powerful symbolic associations of the Roman temple irresistible. According to James Kornwolf, Jefferson regarded the "building's form . . . as an essential part of its function." This becomes clear when we compare it with some earlier Virginia statehouses. For example, the houselike second capitol at Williamsburg (1751–53) had a two-story portico that was added to the front of a building. [Fig. 2-37]

Jefferson wanted a more powerful architecture to express the idea that the people of Virginia are the government, and that they have the right and the responsibility to determine their individual destinies as well as that of the state. The Virginia capitol inspired numerous other statehouses, including the Tennessee Statehouse at Nashville (1845–59) by William Strickland and the new Connecticut Statehouse in New Haven (1827–33), by Town and Davis. [Fig. 2-38]

TEMPLE-INSPIRED COURTHOUSES, TOWN HOUSES, WATER WORKS, AND SCHOOLS

Jefferson's influence on architecture during the first half of the nineteenth century was enormous; the full flowering of his architectural vision is evident in courthouses and town houses throughout the new nation. [Figs. 2-39 and 40] It also permeated new public works projects like the waterworks in Philadelphia, Pennsylvania, and Louisville, Kentucky. [Figs. 2-41 and 42]

FIG. 2-37 *A nineteenth-century view of the sixth Virginia statehouse (1753), the second Capitol built at Williamsburg, initialed E. R. D.*

FIG. 2-38 *Watercolor engraving (mid-nineteenth century) of the New Haven Green showing the Connecticut statehouse (1827–1833) by Town and Davis. The campus of Yale University is on the left and one of the three churches on the Green on the right.*

FIG. 2-39 *Rear view of the Jeffersonian Fluvanna County Courthouse (1831), Palmyra, Virginia.*

ABOVE
FIG. 2-40 *Old Market House (1832), Fayetteville, North Carolina. The Ionic order and arcade may be traced to Jefferson together with Gothic and Puritan influences.*

RIGHT
FIG. 2-41 *The pump houses of the Fairmount Waterworks (1812–1822), Philadelphia, Pennsylvania.*

Following in the path of Jefferson's capitol at Richmond, schools like the Norfolk Academy (1840) in Virginia, designed by Thomas U. Walters, became temples of learning. [Fig. 2-43] Universities followed a similar path, as illustrated by the beautiful Medical College [1836] in Augusta, Georgia, by Charles B. McCluskey. [Fig. 2-44]

A new approach to an old and vexing social problem was tried at Philadelphia's Girard College [1845]. [Fig. 2-45] This complex of five buildings, also planned by Walters, was created to provide a home and education facilities for three hundred orphans. The exterior of the three-story classroom building in the center of the composition was inspired by the form of the ancient Greek temple; the dormitories, on either side, were templelike houses without columns. The brainchild of Stephen Girard, a wealthy local banker, Girard College was surely the noblest set of buildings ever created to serve orphans, a group whose plight in contemporary London was described in graphic detail by Charles Dickens in books like *Oliver Twist* (1839).

OLLE FOR ORPHANS

FIG. 2-45 *Perspective drawing of Girard College (1848), Philadelphia, Pennsylvania, designed by Thomas U. Walters.*

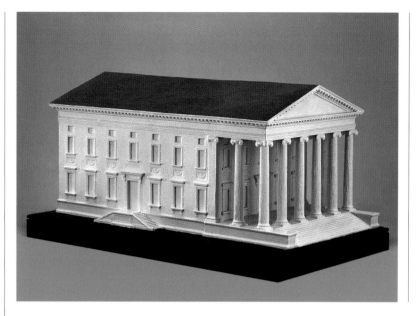

THE LIMITED IMPACT OF THE TEMPLE FORM

Architectural historian Vincent Scully eloquently describes Jefferson as "the greatest classicist in the history of the United States. He ... transform[ed a] ... colonial culture into a national one. He ... use[d] architecture to help create a whole new environment for the nation and to endow it with a new symbolic stance, one that would encourage a truly international culture based upon learning and a new generosity of mind."[29]

Yet the influence of Jefferson's temple model was limited by the inflexibility of its boxlike form. This is aptly illustrated by the Virginia capitol. Jefferson's 1785 model had a monumental front stair leading up to the portico and a door opening directly into the courtroom. [Figs. 2-33, 2-46 and 2-47] The two-story Conference Room—the central public space that provided access to every room in the Capitol—was directly accessible only from the small stairs on either side of the building. The front stair was so unimportant for day-to-day use of the capitol that it was not built in permanent form until the twentieth century.

FIG. 2-46 *Plaster model of the proposed Virginia Capitol commissioned by Jefferson in 1785. It was made in Paris by Jean-Pierre Fouquet and arrived in Richmond in late 1786.*

FIG. 2-47 *Plan of the Virginia Capitol as it is today. Wings were added in 1904 and expanded in 1964. The front room behind the portico was subdivided to accommodate an entry hall for access into the heart of the building.*

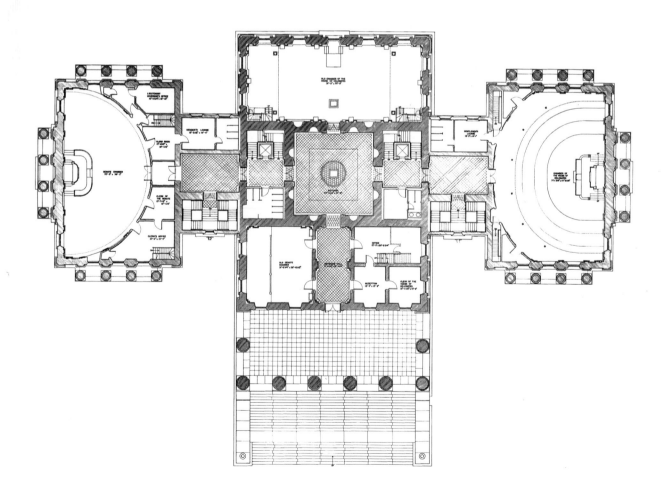

Striving to retain the most significant characteristics of the temple form, early American architects sought ways to transform it into a more flexible instrument. This is demonstrated by the North Carolina Statehouse (1833–40) at Raleigh by Town and Davis. [Fig. 2-48] Inspired by Jefferson's ideas, it is most notable for its innovative cruciform plan. This device enabled its architects to better incorporate all the components of the state house—upper and lower house chambers, governor's office, and supreme court—around the major central space.

The cost and the technical skill required to create such buildings competently also limited the influence of the temple model. The limited economic resources in many small rural and frontier communities encouraged the simple house form as a more practical alternative. [Fig. 2-49]

The completion of the United States Capitol in Washington, D.C., in 1826, offered an exciting and more adaptable architectural model that gradually displaced the influence of the temple form. It is a measure of Jefferson's extraordinary stature as an architect that he also played a critically important role in the creation of this noble building.

FIG. 2-48 *North Carolina Statehouse (1833–1840), Raleigh, North Carolina, designed by Town and Davis.*

FIG. 2-49 *Hinsdale County Courthouse (1877), Lake City, Colorado.*

FIG. 2-50 *The "Tortola Scheme," Dr. William Thornton's first design of 1792 for the competition to design the U. S. Capitol in Washington, D. C.*

FIG. 2-51 *Plan of Thornton's winning design of 1793 for the U. S. Capitol.*

FIG. 2-52 *Benjamin Henry Latrobe's design of 1810 for the east front of the U. S. Capitol.*

THE UNITED STATES CAPITOL IN WASHINGTON, D.C.

*We have built no national temples but the Capitol; we consult
no common oracles but the Constitution.*[30]

— REPRESENTATIVE RUFUS CHOATE OF MASSACHUSETTS, 1833

In 1792, President George Washington initiated a design competition for a United States Congress House in the new federal capital. At the time, the surveyors were busy hammering stakes into the ground to mark the location of the Mall, the sites of the proposed Congress House and President's House, and the streets of the new city. The streets extended across farms, woods, and fields. With characteristic boldness, the president dared to imagine a unique building that would have the first large dome in the New World, a building of "beauty and grandeur."[31] He hoped its architecture would reflect the noble ideals of the new American republic and be the architectural equal of the great palaces and churches of Europe.

A handful of architects (thirteen of whom are known) entered the competition. The prize was awarded to Dr. William Thornton's second design. The current architectural historian of the Capitol, William C. Allen, described Thornton's first design as one that "so resembled a residence that for years it was misidentified as an entry in the President's House [now called the White House] competition."[32] [Fig. 2-50] A few weeks later, Thornton presented a second, very different scheme. This entry immediately captured the imagina-

tion of both President Washington and Secretary of State Jefferson. [Fig. 2-51] On February 1, 1793, Jefferson wrote that "Dr. Thornton's plan of a capitol has captivated the eyes and judgment of all. . . . It is simple, noble, beautiful . . . and among its admirers no one is more delighted than him [President Washington]."[33] It was deemed the winner, and construction began in July. This design was the largest building in the new nation and its plan was complex.

After Jefferson became president, he appointed Benjamin Henry Latrobe as the first architect of the Capitol, while retaining Thornton as an advisor. Latrobe, in collaboration with Jefferson, designed remarkable room interiors and exterior façades for Thornton's design. [Fig. 2-52] President Monroe insisted on modifying Latrobe's design by making the dome taller to emphasize its symbolic significance. His instruction was reluctantly carried out by Latrobe's successor, Charles Bulfinch, who tried in vain to convince the president to retain the design of the dome so admired by Washington and Jefferson. The building was completed in 1826. [Fig. 2-53]

In 1826, the Capitol was a rectangular building with an entrance portico in the middle of the eastern side and a colonnade on the west. There were additional entrances on the northern and southern façades. In the center of the building, beneath the dome, marking the crossing of the two main axes, was a large, round hall. [Fig. 2-54] Modeled after the Roman Pantheon, Jefferson and Latrobe designated this great room the Hall of the People. President Washington intended that the Hall of the People be the most magnificent room in the new nation. Significantly, it was not assigned to the Senate,

FIG. 2-53 *"West Front of the Capitol of the United States," painted by Charles Burton and presented to the Marquis de Lafayette to commemorate his visit to the Capitol in 1824. It shows the taller dome designed according to the instruction of President Monroe.*

to the House of Representatives, or to the president. It was intended as a place for citizens—for the government—to gather to discuss the legislation that would shape the nation's future. This momentous architectural decision is the material embodiment of the opening sentences of the Constitution: "*We, the People* of the United States, in Order to form a more perfect Union . . . do ordain and establish this Constitution for the United States of America." The establishment of the nation and the formulation of its Constitution and government were enacted by and for the people. This same truth had been stated twenty-three years earlier in the Declaration of Independence. It is the "people" who declare: "When in the Course of human events, it becomes necessary for one people to dissolve the political bands which have connected them with another," and the People who "hold these truths to be self-evident, that

all men are created equal." The Hall of the People may be described as the nation's living room.[34] And it is appropriate that its circular defining wall is decorated with paintings that depict the founding of the republic. [Fig. 2-54]

Representatives and senators, servants of the people, have chambers in secondary locations on the Capitol's cross axis on either side of the Hall of the People. [Fig. 2-55] The president, also a servant of the people, is located in a separate building at 1600 Pennsylvania Avenue, the White House. [Fig. 2-56] Washington, who served as president of the Constitutional Convention, carefully defined this relationship in a letter written in 1787 to his nephew and future Supreme Court justice, Bushrod Washington:

The power under the Constitution will always be with *the people*. It is entrusted for certain defined purposes and for a certain limited period, to representa-

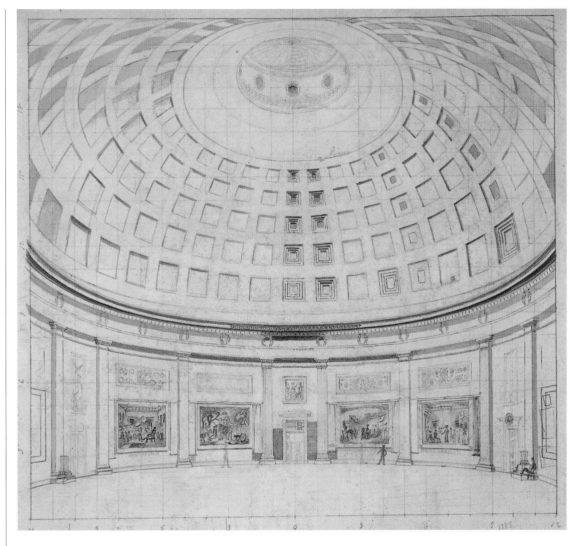

LEFT

FIG. 2-54 *A "Perspective View of Capitol Rotunda," drawn by Alexander Jackson Davis in 1832. The interior illustrates Latrobe's design for the Hall of the People.*

BOTTOM LEFT

FIG. 2-55 *Latrobe's design in 1806 for the "Principal Story of the Capitol, U. S."*

BOTTOM RIGHT

FIG. 2-56 *View of the east front of the President's House. Lithography by E. Sachse & Co. 1860.*

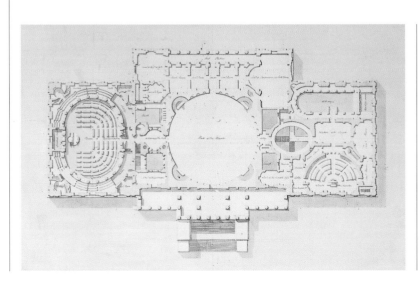

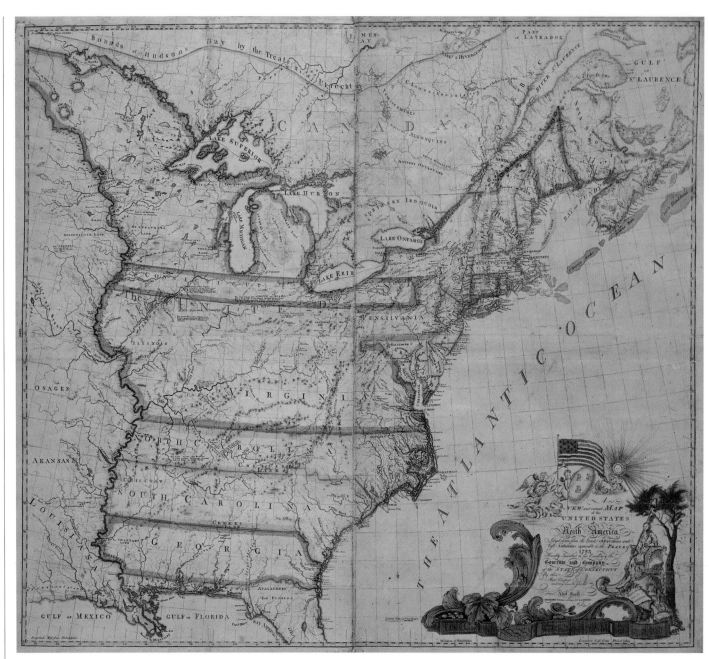

FIG. 2-57 *Abel Buell,* A New and correct Map of the United States of North America Layd down from the latest Observations and best Authority agreeable to the Peace of 1783. *This was engraved in 1784 and was the first map of the new nation.*

tives of their own choosing; and whenever it is executed contrary to their interests, or not agreeable to their wishes, *their Servants* can, and undoubtedly will be, recalled. [emphasis added][35]

Nearly 150 years later, President Theodore Roosevelt echoed this thought when he stated that "the president is merely the most important among a large number of public Servants."[36]

These political beliefs are expressed symbolically in both the plan of Washington, D.C., and the architecture of the Capitol. The Constitution called

for a new capital city. Washington proposed a site at the new nation's geographic center—the approximate midpoint between the nation's northern and southern boundaries in 1787—that was accepted by Congress. [Fig. 2-57] The Capitol building sits on a hill at the very center of the city and shares its major axes. [Fig. 2-58] The circular form of the Hall of the People, marked in space by the great dome, is the symbolic center of the capital city and of the nation. From here, twelve avenues radiate out through the surrounding city and, metaphorically, to the far corners of the country, inviting citizens to visit their public living

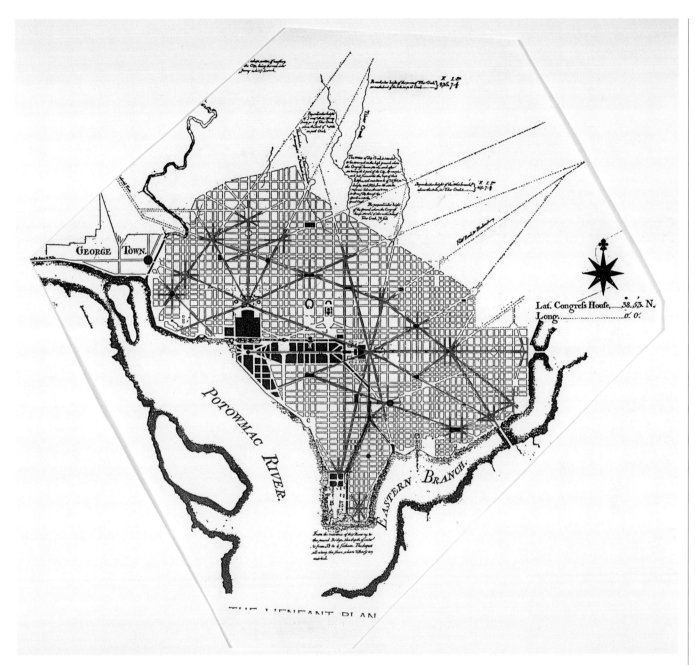

FIG. 2-58 *Peter Charles L'Enfant,* Plan of the City intended for the Permanent Seat of the Government of the United States *(1791).*

room in the heart of their nation's capital. [Fig. 2-59] This makes the Hall of the People the most important space in the building and the political center of the capital city and the nation. This idea was powerfully expressed in a speech given in 1909 by President William Howard Taft:

> [George] Washington intended this to be a Federal City, and it is a Federal City, and it tingles down to the feet of everyman, whether he comes from Washington State, Los Angeles, or Texas, when he comes and walks these city streets and begins to feel that this is my city; I own a part of this Capital.[37]

In 1855, Thomas U. Walters prepared plans to enlarge the Capitol building. He also redesigned the dome as a much taller and more dramatic structure. This modification suggests its symbolism even more emphatically. [Fig. 2-60] Construction of the new dome was completed during the Civil War. President Abraham Lincoln took the opportunity provided by the ongoing construction during the war to expand the meaning of the dome to symbolize the struggle to preserve the Union. The enlarged building is also remarkable for its numerous entrances, which invite citizens to enter, and for the large

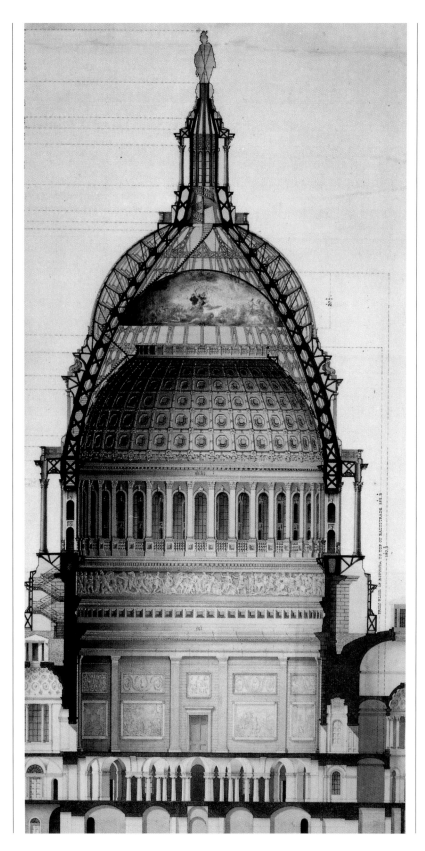

FIG. 2-59 *An 1859 cross-section of the proposed new dome of the U.S. Capitol and the Hall of the People by Thomas U. Walters.*

public galleries in the new House and Senate chambers. Whether seen from the Mall or the surrounding city, the great dome of the Capitol dominates the horizon and pulsates with the message: The government is the people. [Fig. 2-61]

The architecture of the Capitol is very different from the Puritan ideal of the citizen's house as a model for public buildings. Washington and Jefferson were likely concerned that the Puritans' vision, with its emphasis on local tradition, may have reinforced differences between the states and encouraged national fragmentation. They looked to the architecture of federal buildings, and to the symbolism their forms projected, as one way to help unify the independent states of colonial times into a single nation. Most of us have forgotten that quite soon after the great military victory at Yorktown, the states began squabbling among themselves. Their seeming lack of binding interests, especially economic ones, threatened to undermine the stability of the new nation.

It is not clear if Washington and Jefferson imagined that many states would adopt the monumental vocabulary of the Capitol for their statehouses, or if they assumed that regional government buildings would continue to develop local traditions of domestic design. Yet the pediment, imbued with its renewed symbolism, is an important architectural feature of the late colonial home, the meetinghouse, the Maryland Statehouse, the Virginia Capitol, and the United States Capitol. And these different edifices reflected a belief in the power of architecture to communicate political ideas and represent ideals.

THE STATEHOUSE BASED ON THE MODEL OF THE CAPITOL

Following the example of the U.S. Capitol, Charles Bulfinch designed the new Massachusetts Statehouse (1795) in Boston. Its bold colonnade introduced a new scale and sophistication of architectural design to New England. The tall dome dominated Boston's skyline and for many years the Statehouse was the first building seen by ships approaching the harbor. [Fig. 2-62] Other states soon followed this example. [Fig. 2-63] So pervasive was the authority of the Capitol's design that it even influenced the plan and exterior silhouette of the unusual Gothic Revival Connecticut Statehouse (1872) in Hartford. [Fig. 2-64] The architect, Richard M. Upjohn, located the upper and lower houses on

FIG. 2-60 *Rotunda, United States Capitol with new dome by Thomas U. Walters.*

FIG. 2-61 *View from the Mall of the West Front of the United States Capitol.*

either side of a dramatic multistory central space. Akin to a Hall of the People, it provides circulation and meeting areas for citizens and their elected representatives. [Fig. 2-65] An unusual domed tower caps this great room. [Fig. 2-66]

At the end of the nineteenth century there was an important shift of sensibility, or perhaps a loss of conviction. This is illustrated by the statehouses of Rhode Island (1891-1903) by McKim, Mead & White and of Minnesota (1895–1905) by Cass Gilbert. [Figs. 2-67 and 2-68] Although inspired by the Capitol in Washington, both buildings subtly undercut the central idea of the Capitol's design: that the dominant central space is the Hall of the People. At

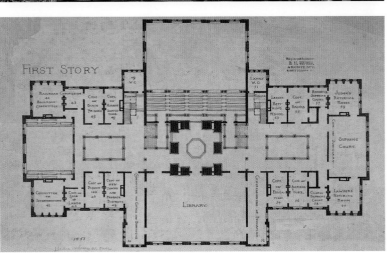

FIG. 2-64 *Connecticut Statehouse (1872–1879), Hartford, Connecticut, designed by Richard M. Upjohn.*

FIG. 2-65 *Plan of the first floor of the Connecticut Statehouse.*

FIG. 2-66 *Interior view up and into the Connecticut Statehouse rotunda.*

FIG. 2-67 *Rhode Island State Capitol, 1891–1903), Providence, Rhode Island, designed by McKim, Mead, & White.*

FIG. 2-68 *Minnesota State Capitol (1895–1905), St. Paul, Minnesota, designed by Cass Gilbert.*

FIG. 2-69 *Interior of the space under the rotunda of the Rhode Island State Capitol.*

FIG. 2-70 *North Dakota State Capitol (1920–1934), Bismarck, North Dakota, designed by Holabird and Root.*

Providence, a monumental stair occupies the space under the dome. At St. Paul, there is a large circular opening in the main floor between the house and senate chambers. It is a spatial extension of the entrance floor below. In neither building is the area under the dome a Hall of the People, a fully realized gathering space for citizens. [Fig. 2-69]

Another, perhaps more serious, illustration of this loss of conviction occurs at the North Dakota State Capitol Building (1920–34) in Bismarck. [Fig. 2-70] First, there is no Hall of the People. The area has been transformed into a wide corridor that connects House, Senate, Supreme Court chambers. Second, the exterior design lacks symbolism. [Fig. 2-71] A taller mass and connected lower structure, the Bismark Statehouse looks like an important office

FIG. 2-71 *North Dakota State Capitol exterior.*

FIG. 2-72 *North Carolina Legislative Building (1963), Raleigh, North Carolina, designed by Edward Durrell Stone.*

building. The new North Carolina State Legislative Building (1963) in Raleigh, designed by Edward Durrell Stone, is indistinguishable from a corporate building or a concert hall. [Fig. 2-72] By the middle of the twentieth century, the intellectual and emotional symbolism that related our American architecture to the spirit of democracy had been abandoned.

COURTHOUSES AFTER RATIFICATION OF THE CONSTITUTION

After ratification of the Constitution, the courthouse took on a new significance in the life of the nation. A courthouse was not only the place to which citizens came to seek justice; it also became the venue in which legal and constitutional rights could be upheld and the actions of congress and the president tested for their constitutionality.

As the nation's population grew and the frontier pushed west, the presence of a courthouse in a town embodied the rule of law. The building was a prominent locus of social and political life. Civil, criminal, and constitutional conflicts were determined in the courtrooms; and births, marriages, and deaths were recorded in the office of the clerk. The judge and clerk of the court were respected members of town society. The clerk was also the archivist responsible for recording land claims and ownership, and storing surveys that showed property divisions. So important was this responsibility that Henry Russell Hitchcock and William Seale described the courthouse archive as the "ark of men's covenant with the land." For successive generations of immigrants, land claims were "sacred."[39] They were the documents that established them as landowners—an unimaginable status for most who chose to leave their native lands—and as citizens of a democratic republic in which they had unprecedented access to social, political, and economic opportunity.

SYMBOLISM IN COURTHOUSE ARCHITECTURE

The courthouse was often regarded as the most important building in the community, prominently sited in relation to a central square. [Figs. 2-73 and 2-74] For most of the nineteenth and early twentieth centuries, citizens and judges went to great lengths to ensure that visitors could easily identify the local courthouse. Because these courthouses were the third and coequal branch of government, the entrance façade often had a pediment or arch.

FIG. 2-73 *Federal Courthouse and Post Office (c. 1913), New Haven, Connecticut, designed by James Gamble Rogers.*

FIG. 2-74 *Courthouse (1912), in the center of Philipsburg, Montana.*

FACING PAGE
FIG. 2-75 *Old St. Louis Courthouse (1839–1862), St. Louis, Missouri.*

While there was usually only one statehouse and one governor's mansion, the judicial branch of government was a pervasive presence in most cities and towns.

The more expansive and flexible design model of the United States Capitol was quickly recognized as an obvious exemplar for local, state, and federal courthouses. [Fig. 2-75] Its authority is even evident in courthouses that ignore the federal architectural style of the Capitol, such as the magnificent Romanesque Revival design of the Allegheny County Courthouse (1883–1888) in Pittsburgh, designed by Henry Hobson Richardson. [Fig. 2-76]

In place of a centrally located Hall of the People, Richardson planned the major public gathering spaces on each floor in relation to the monumental open stair in the front of the building. A monumental tower was built directly above this stair. At the time of its construction, the tower was an important and prominent symbol on the city's skyline.

Symbolism was an essential component in planning courthouses. The lobby was meant to serve a role similar to that of the Hall of the People in the United States Capitol: a central gathering space for citizens. It could serve as a waiting room, a place for attorneys to meet informally with

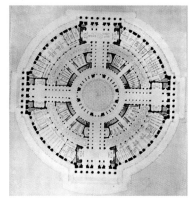

CLOCKWISE FROM TOP LEFT

FIG. 2-76 *Allegheny County Courthouse (1883–1888), Pittsburgh, Pennsylvania designed by H. H. Richardson.*

FIG. 2-77 *Courthouse lobby (1821–1822), Monroe County, Rochester, New York.*

FIG. 2-78 *Plan of the winning design for the proposed New York Courthouse in 1913, designed by Guy Lowell.*

FIG. 2-79 *Courtroom in the Allegheny County Courthouse.*

clients, and a means of direct access to courtrooms, offices, and other court facilities. [Figs. 2-77 and 2-78] The symbolic importance of the courthouse lobby was understood to be so fundamental that it became the organizing principle around which the entire building was planned. In larger cities, where expanding populations required many more courtrooms and offices, these central lobbies became magnificent, multistory, vaulted rooms. They were not expressions of the grandeur of the court system or the state; rather they were dedicated to the service of the public and to the principle that "We, the People" are the cornerstone of the nation's government.

THE ROLE OF SYMBOLISM IN COURTROOM DESIGN

Symbolism was an even more critical element in the layout of courtrooms. The formal placement of the various participants in the trial was, and is still, "a direct reflection of society's view of the appropriate relationship between an individual accused of a crime and judicial authority."[40] It is an expression of our adversarial system of justice. [Figs. 2-79 and 2-81] The judge is located in the center of the front of the courtroom to symbolize the role of unbiased arbiter between two contending parties: the defense and the prosecution representing the state. Because they are in opposition but are equal in status, the parties sit at similar

FIG. 2-81 *City Hall (1803–1811), New York, New York, designed by Mangin and McComb.*

FIG. 2-80 *Layout showing the location of the participants in a typical American courtroom.*

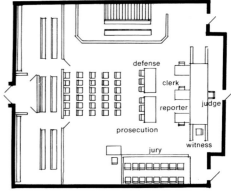

BELOW
FIG. 2-82 *Old City Hall (1820), Washington, D.C., designed by George Hadfield.*

FACING PAGE
FIG. 2-83 *City Hall (1883), Albany, New York, designed by H. H. Richardson.*

tables set out symmetrically, facing the judge's bench. The defendant, innocent until proven guilty, sits at the defense table with counsel. The public, at the rear of the courtroom, faces the judge and observes the law in action. The jurors, who determine guilt or innocence, are placed on one side of the courtroom. They are unbiased observers, removed from the axis of judge, counsel, defendant, and public. Because defendants are entitled to confront their accusers, the witnesses face the counsel tables but are placed adjacent to, and under the protection of, the judge.

This courtroom layout is not an arbitrary arrangement of furniture; it symbolizes our concern with protecting the rights of a person accused of a crime. In this context, it should be noted that courtrooms in other countries are very different and relate to their particular legal systems. In England, for example, an accused person sits alone with a guard in the "dock," a small, secure seating area that faces the judge's bench and is raised up above the rest of the courtroom.

THE CITY HALL AND FIREHOUSE

Because of the importance of local government, city halls are often powerful works of architecture. This may have been a result of the charisma of the

COUNTERCLOCKWISE
FROM TOP LEFT
FIG. 2-84 *City Hall (1893),
Spring City, Utah.*

FIG. 2-85 *Engine Company
No. 1 (c. 1900),
Alexandria, Virginia.*

FIG. 2-86 *Firehouse (1884),
New York, New York.*

FACING PAGE
TOP
FIG. 2-87 *Fire Station #3
(1903), Seattle, Washington.*

BOTTOM
FIG. 2-88 *Fire Station (1928),
Santa Barbara, California,
designed by Edwards, Plunkett,
and Howell, Architects.*

mayor as well as the more flexible character of local government. Communities in many major urban centers wished to shed all vestiges of the colonial past and to manifest their optimism about the future. This may explain why the term *town house* was forgotten. Two remarkable examples of new city halls are in New York (1803–11) by Mangin & McComb and in Washington D.C. (1820), designed by George Hadfield. [Figs. 2-80 and 2-82] As the century progressed, urban city halls tended to be responsive to the latest architectural trends. [Fig. 2-83] In smaller rural towns and frontier settlements the town hall retained the older ideal of a more houselike building for economic reasons. In some cases an actual house was used. [Fig. 2-84]

Firehouse architecture in the nineteenth and early twentieth centuries is largely uncelebrated. The extensive use of wood for construction made towns and settlements particularly vulnerable to fire. What began as *ad hoc* citizen bucket brigades were formalized into volunteer fire companies—still active in many rural and suburban communities—and full-time fire companies in cities. [Fig. 2-85] The architects of the buildings that house the firefighters and their equipment generally strove for compatibility of scale and character with the surrounding neighborhood. This resulted in remarkable and innovative design. This is well-illustrated by firehouses in Old Town Alexandria, Virginia, New York, Seattle, and Santa Barbara. [Fig. 2-86, 2-87, and 2-88]

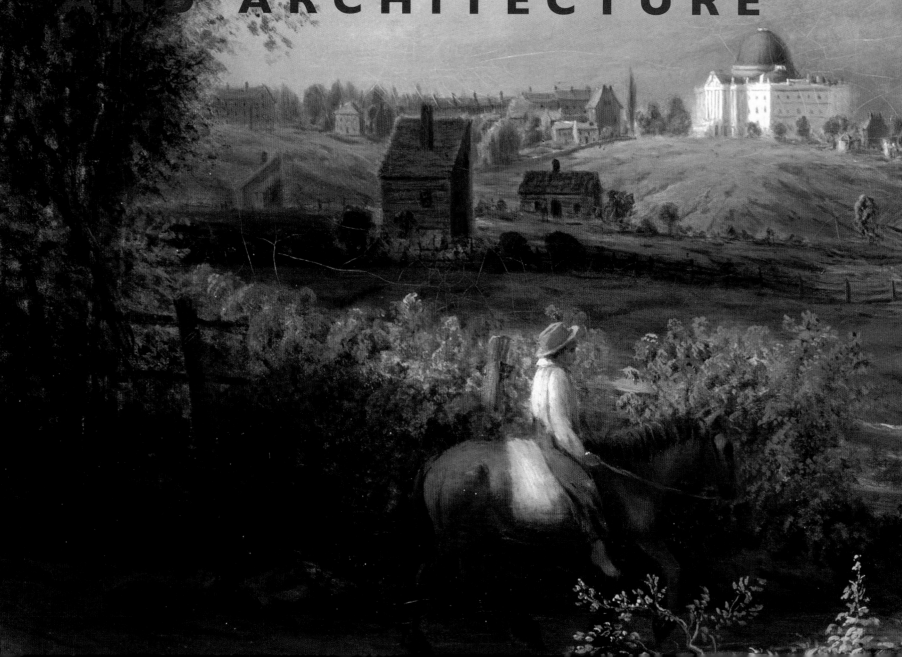

DEMOCRACY, ANTHROPOMORPHISM, AND ARCHITECTURE

... human beings fashion an environment for themselves, a space to live in, [that is] suggested by their patterns of life and constructed around whatever symbols of reality seem important to them. Most of all, that environment and those structures invest the vast indifference of nature with meanings intelligible to, indeed imagined by, mankind, and they involve ... all those complex relationships of human buildings with each other that shape within nature a new manmade topography ... [1]

— VINCENT SCULLY,
ARCHITECTURE: THE NATURAL AND THE MAN MADE

Archibald MacLeish described the United States as a "self-constituted, self-declared, self-created" nation.[2] This differentiates its citizens from, say, Spaniards or Danes, whose national identities were forged though a shared birthright of language, religion, culture, and occupation of the same region, sometimes for millennia. To become an American was different. It was, and remains, a decision based on choices: to leave one's country of birth, to cross an ocean or border, and to start a new life in a new land. For the English colonists, as well as later generations of immigrants, it offered a way to escape the fetters of religious persecution, class barriers, and economic privation. After the revolution, coming to the United States offered an opportunity to join a nation of immigrants, to seek a better life by embracing the political ideals and principles outlined in the Constitution, Declaration of Independence, and Bill of Rights. That remains true today, as one in every eight or nine people living in the United States is an immigrant—legal or otherwise.

A small number of other Americans, like the great novelist Henry James, decried the leveling nature of a democratic society. Born into a privileged New York City family, James preferred to live in England. Writing in 1879, he lamented that the United States had "no sovereign, no court, no personal loyalty, no aristocracy, no church, no clergy, no army, no diplomatic service, no country

gentlemen, no palaces, no castles, nor manors, nor old country houses, nor parsonages, nor thatched cottages, nor ivied ruins; no cathedrals, nor abbeys, nor little Norman churches; no great Universities, nor public schools—no Oxford, nor Eton, nor Harrow; no literature, no novels, no museums, no pictures, no political societies, no sporting class—no Epson nor Ascot!"[3]

Such elitist sentiment may be unusual in a society of staunch democratic individualism. As the Israeli scholar A. B. Yehoshua notes,

> it still seems that for us democracy is like wearing a suit of clothes after trying on various other styles, while for Americans it is more than a suit or a coat—it is like the very skin of their body. That is because, if I am not mistaken, the United States is the only nation in the world whose national identity is almost genetically related to democracy. Its national independence was forged at birth within the world of democratic presuppositions.[4]

That idea was put forward as early as 1835 by Alexis de Tocqueville, who wrote that he considered social "mores to be one of the great general causes to which the maintenance of a democratic republic in the United States can be attributed."[5]

TOWARD A NEW ARCHITECTURE

Given the lack of cultural traditions, including architectural ones, how could the new nation establish an identity? Understanding that architecture is an expression of political power, Washington and Jefferson believed that the new nation's public buildings could articulate the particular and unique form of political authority enshrined in the Constitution, Declaration of Independence,

FIG. 3-3 *The Pantheon (126 AD), Rome, Italy.*

FIG. 3-4 *Entrance to Wilton House (1753), Richmond, Virginia.*

and Bill of Rights. [Fig. 3-1] Washington and Jefferson utilized architecture as public expression to differentiate their new democratic political culture from that of England, a constitutional monarchy since 1688, and the other European monarchies, which retained rigid systems of class and economic privilege.

What were the particular political ideas enshrined in the founding documents around which a new architecture of democracy could be developed? First, the Declaration of Independence proclaimed a new and revolutionary goal: the creation of a government explicitly for the purpose of securing the "life, liberty, and pursuit of happiness" of its citizens. Neither a theocratic government nor a nation of subjects serving their king, it was to be a nation of free citizens seeking their own welfare and deciding their own future. Second, embedded in the opening phrase of the Constitution is the statement: "We, the People of the United States, in order to form a more perfect Union . . ." In 1793 Supreme Court Justice James Wilson explained the significance of those words: "the people . . . of the United States . . . have reserved the supreme power in their own hands; and on that supreme power, have made the state [nation] dependent."[6] That wording had been debated at the Constitutional Convention in Philadelphia in 1787–88. A counter-suggestion, endorsed by Virginia radical Patrick Henry, was that the opening phrase should be "We, the States," suggesting a very different form of government, one in which state legislatures were the dominant forces. Gouverneur Morris, a delegate of Pennsylvania, insisted on the words "We, the people," which underscored the principle that citizens—not states—constitute this nation. Justice Wilson further noted that while much had been "written concerning the prerogatives of kings, and concerning the sovereignty of states . . . little has been said and written, concerning a subject much more dignified and important, the *majesty of the people*."

Although the Declaration of Independence was written to be presented to King George III, the founding documents—all written with remarkable clarity, concision, and modesty—are addressed to the citizenry. And that citizenry understood the revolutionary implications of the principles embedded in the texts. According to the founding documents, the individual—human being, citizen, and voter—is the basic building block of the nation, the fundamental unit of the larger, aggregate citizens' government. It was the "majesty of the people" that Washington and Jefferson wished to express in the new nation's public buildings. In doing so, they recognized the particular quality of political authority that the architecture should embody. And they believed in the power of architecture to distinguish and articulate the unique aspects of the new nation and the life of its citizens.

How was that achieved? The approach used by Washington, Jefferson, and other architects in the federal period was to *modify the meaning and symbolism of existing architectural forms to articulate new meanings*. The essential component of this method was a discourse between new requirements and past precedent, much like the method used to draft the Constitution. Like the philosophers of antiquity who searched for universal principles, so the members of the Constitutional Convention strove to structure the Constitution on principles that would endure. The application of older ideas—drawn from classical antiquity and contemporary England, France, Holland, and Italy—to a new democratic form of government resulted in a completely fresh formulation of familiar principles and ideals. It was through that process that a complete reshaping of traditional political forms could be made explicit. The result was a Constitution that was both ancient and modern. It was precisely in this vein that Jefferson described the Declaration of Independence. Its goal was:

Not to find out new principles, or new arguments, never before thought of, not merely to say things which had never been said before. . . . Neither aiming at originality of principle or sentiment, nor yet copied from any particular and previous writing, it was simply intended to be an expression of the American mind . . . . All its authority rests then on the harmonizing sentiments of the day, whether expressed in conversation, in letters, printed essays, or in the elementary books of public right, as Aristotle, Cicero, Locke, Sidney, &c.[7]

THE TRANSFORMATION OF SYMBOLS IN ARCHITECTURE

In architecture we find a similar process at work. The colonists understood that the use of a portico and pediment to express royal authority in the palace of a king derived from the architecture of the ancient Greek and Roman temple. [Figs. 3-2 and 3-3] By appropriating the front of the classical temple in the design of the doorways to their own homes, early Americans adapted their houses to reflect a very different form of political reality. Set over columns or pilasters framing the front door of a citizen's house, a pediment tells us that in this new nation the rights and prerogatives that were once reserved for the gods of the ancient world—and later for the kings of Europe—now belong to ordinary citizens. [Fig. 3-4] Those modest houses may have been one of the most radical political statements ever expressed in architectural form. They were created through a dialogue between precedent and the new political and practical demands of life in colonial and federal North America. Designed by owners or builders without professional training, they illustrate how the homes of ordinary citizens became works of architecture for the first time in history.[8] They are living illustrations of the way in which the Constitution empowered citizens to determine their own destinies as well as those of their communities and the nation.

Architects today reject the use of forms imbued with symbolism. It is therefore salutary to consider a particularly poignant project that celebrates the transformative power of symbols. At 4 a.m. on July 4, 1976, a young graduate of Yale's School of Architecture, Carl Wies, nailed in place a bold and unique contribution to New Haven's Bicentennial celebration. He had painstakingly designed a new façade for an unsightly temporary trailer used by the state's Juvenile Court. Set between the city's library and the state courthouse, the trailer structure presented an incongruous spectacle on the city's 338-year old green. [Fig. 3-5a] He drew the façade on Styrofoam boards that he singlehandedly nailed in place just before sunrise; the city awoke to a delightful surprise. [Fig. 3-5b] Such was the power of the classical design that the state spurned an offer from a civic-minded citizen to transfer his work to a more permanent medium that would last for the life of the construction. Why was this offer rejected? First, there was concern that the citizens of New Haven would grow so fond of the new façade they would have resisted the eventual removal of the trailers; and second, that this design would set a standard and establish an alternative direction that new state buildings in New Haven, as well as other cities in the state, would be unable to match. For the modernist architects serving with state and local public works departments, this option appeared to be a form of heresy.

What, we might ask, was the powerful attraction of the classical past for the American revolutionaries who were searching for ways to transform and adapt its forms and symbols? The answer is a critically important idea that lies at the core of democratic Athens and the Roman republic: their *anthropocentric culture* and their *anthropomorphic* architecture. Although neither society was able to realize its ideals in full, both initiated a political philosophy that strove for an enduring human-centered culture and form of government. Nearly seventeen hundred years later, colonists in America initiated a revolution in order to reestablish *anthropocentric* culture through the founding of a

FIG. 3-5a *Temporary Juvenile Court (1975), New Haven, Connecticut.*

FIG. 3-5b *Carl Wies's new façade nailed on to the Temporary Juvenile Court on July 4, 1976.*

new and stronger democratic form of government. That is why late colonial, federal, nineteenth- and early twentieth-century Americans, and their architects, were preoccupied with the process of transforming architectural symbols through a dialogue between past and contemporary requirements. It is why, within the rubric of their dreams of democracy, they looked to the *anthropomorphism* that constituted the core of classical architecture to help them develop an architecture that embodied democratic ideals.

Architectural anthropomorphism is the attribution of human form and qualities to architectural forms.[9] [Fig. 3-6] In Athens, that idea was part of the anthropocentric—that is, human-centered—idea of democracy.[10] The political and architectural expressions of the ancient Greek anthropocentric world were inseparable. The architecture of the American Revolution marked the first time since the fall of democratic Athens that these two ideas were again combined.

ANTHROPOMORPHIC ARCHITECTURE

How do architectural forms become anthropomorphic? The process demands an imaginative leap to connect the accumulated memories of our body's struggle to maintain stability as we stand, climb, bend, fall, and move objects—that is, as we resist and accommodate the forces of gravity and inertia—and our experience of stability and instability of architectural forms. According to Geoffrey Scott, the English architectural theorist, we relate those experiences to architecture by empathy.[11] Thus when we ascribe human attributes to a column or a building, empathy facilitates the translation into human terms. For example, the word façade, the front or elevation of a building, is rooted in the Vulgar Latin *faccia*, or the Latin *facies*, both of which mean face.[12] We may also transcribe our image of ourselves in terms of architecture by imagining that we are a building or parts of a building, like columns.

To the Greeks, columns were metaphors for human beings. Thus a Doric column was a man; an Ionic column, a woman; and a Corinthian column, a maiden. [Figs. 3-7a and b, and 3-8a and b] Using ancient Greek sources, the ancient Roman architect and writer Vitruvius gave us the following description of the origin of the Doric column:

> Wishing to set up columns in that temple [to Apollo] . . . and being in search of some way by which they could render them fit to bear a load and also of a satisfactory beauty of appearance, they measure the imprint of a man's foot and compared it with his height. On finding that in a man, the foot is one sixth of the height, they applied the same principle to the column, and reared the shaft, including the capital, to a height six times its thickness at its base. Thus the Doric column, as used in buildings, begins to exhibit the proportions, strength, and beauty of the body of a man.[13]

Writing about the Ionic order, he described how the Greeks "translated . . . the slenderness of women" by making the thickness of the column "one eighth of its height." He noted that "at the foot they substituted a base in place of a shoe; in the capital they placed the volutes, hanging down at the right and the

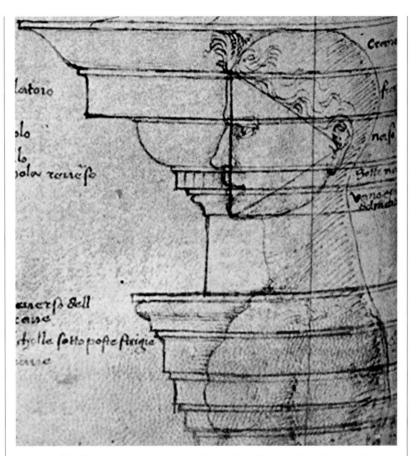

FIG. 3-6 *Detail of an anthropomorphic entablature from* Trattato di architettura di Francesco di Giorgio Martini, Il Codice Ashburnham 361 della Biblioteca Medicea Laurenziana di Firenze *showing an anthropomorphic entablature.*

left like curly ringlets, and ornamented its front with cymatia [a molding with an S-shaped profile] and festoons of fruit arranged in place of hair, while they brought the flutes down the whole shaft, falling like the folds in the robes worn by matrons." He summarized the process by noting that "in the invention of the two different kinds of columns they borrowed manly beauty, naked and unadorned, for the one, and for the other the delicacy, adornment, and proportions characteristic of women."[14]

At the Erechtheum, also on the Acropolis, the columns are carved into literal representations of human beings. These female figures with Ionic capitals above their heads are called *caryatids*. [Fig. 3-9] The Doric columns that surround the Parthenon, the dwelling of the goddess Athena on the Acropolis, are metaphoric Athenian men supporting the roof of her house. At the Lincoln Memorial in Washington, D.C., the columns are citizens of the states of the Union standing in honor of the memory of their president. [Fig. 3-10]

The anthropomorphic qualities of the ancient Greek column are expressed in the base, the tampering shaft, and the capital, which correspond to the human foot, body, and head. The tamper of the shaft is a subtle curve

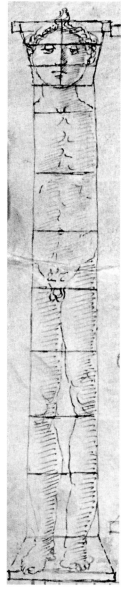

FROM LEFT TO RIGHT

FIG. 3-7a *Corner column, Parthenon (477–438 BC), Athens, Greece.*

FIG. 3-7b *Plate from* Trattato di architettura di Francesco di Giorgio Martini, Il Codice Ashburnham 361 della Biblioteca Medicea Laurenziana di Firenze *illustrating the anthropomorphic basis of a Doric column.*

FIG. 3-8a *Ionic Column of the Portico of Tiberius (mid-second century), Aphrodisias, Turkey.*

FIG. 3-8b *Sketch based on a drawing from* Trattato di architettura di Francesco di Giorgio Martini, Il Codice Saluzziana 148, Biblioteca reale di Torino *illustrating the anthropomorphic basis of an Ionic column.*

called *entasis*. [Fig. 3-11] It refers to the human need to stand with feet apart, wider than the torso, in order to comfortably balance a load and be stable. The overall proportions of both columns and buildings may be derived from the relationships of the parts of the human body. The anthropomorphic classical column establishes a direct link between human beings and buildings. [Fig. 3-12] In that regard they can be easily distinguished from the post, an unarticulated round or rectangular structural member. [Fig. 3-13] Entasis has also been explained as an "optical refinement" developed by the Greeks to counteract the "disagreeable optical illusion" by which columns with straight sides appear "attenuated" with "concave sides."[15]

The anthropomorphic column worked in conjunction with the pediment to create the dwelling of a Greek or Roman god. Some Renaissance architects, like Francesco di Giorgio, proposed that the human figure should be the basis of church architecture. The plan he suggested was structured around a body

FIG. 3-9 *Caryatid Porch at the Erechtheion (421-406 BC), Athens, Greece.*

FIG. 3-10 *Doric colonnade at the Lincoln Memorial, (1912–1922), Washington, D.C., designed by Henry Bacon.*

with arms outstretched. [Fig. 3-14] Architectural historian Henry Millon recognized the close correspondence between one of Francesco's drawings and the façade of Santa Maria della Grazie (1484), a church he designed in the village of Calcinaio.[16] [Figs. 3-15a and b] The pediment is the head and the rectangular walls form the body; horizontal divisions are related to navel, pelvis, and knees. That was appropriate "as the body has all its members proportioned and subdivided according to perfect measure."[17] This Renaissance notion was

an outgrowth of St. Augustine's belief that the human body's formal and functional beauty was such that it must be accorded primacy in God's creation of the world.[18] Man was created in God's image, as described in Genesis 1:26; it therefore stands at the peak of physical creation. According to architectural historian Lawrence Lowic, Francesco do Giorgio employs "particular geometric figures" that Lowic believes "embody the principles of arrangement and measurement generic to the human body."[19] Filarete, another Renaissance

FIG. 3-11 Trattato di architettura di Francesco di Giorgio Martini, Il Codice Ashburnham 361 della Biblioteca Medicea Laurenziana di Firenze *illustrating entasis.*

FIG. 3-12 *John Shute's study of the Doric order from his book* The First and Chief Groundes of Architecture used in all the ancient and famous monymentes *(1563).*

FIG. 3-13 *A round structural post supporting an office building in Washington, D.C.*

FIG. 3-14 *Pietro Cataneo's anthropomorphic drawing of a church plan from his book* L'architettura *(1567).*

writer on architecture, went one step further. He cited Adam trying to protect himself from the rain by placing his hands overlapped on his head with elbows pointing sideways as the origin of the roof. [Fig. 3-16] Adam's body would have represented the walls of the house. Filarete described it in the following terms:

> It must therefore be believed that Adam, having made himself a roof with his two hands, considered the need for making a living, he reflected and exercised himself to make some habitation to defend himself from the rains, as well as from the heat of he sun.[20]

Nicholas Cusanus, one of the most original speculative thinkers of the Renaissance, went so far as to relate the structure of the state, including the relationship between secular and religious authorities, to the human body. He likened the body and its joints to parts of buildings. Thus both structures and walls are slightly wider at the bottom than at the top to suggest the stability we feel with our feet apart. Their plinths, like the ankle, are a transition between superstructure and foundation; they articulate the transition from the

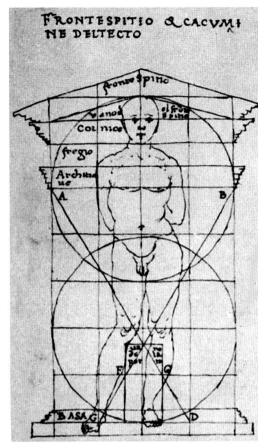

FRONTESPITIO & CACVMI
NE DELTECTO

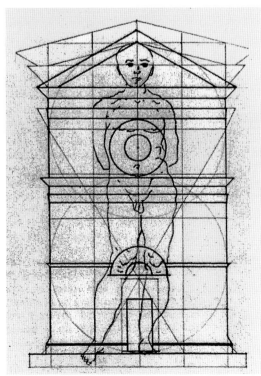

FIG. 3-15a *Francesco di Giorgio's study of the anthropomorphic façade of his design for S. Maria delle Grazie al Calcinaio, Cortona, from Cod. Magli. II, 141.*

FIG. 3-15b *Henry Millon's comparison between Francesco di Giorgio's drawing of a church façade and its relationship to a human figure and the façade of Francesco's Santa Maria della Erayle (1484).*

FIG. 3-16 *Filarete's drawing of Adam cast out from the Garden of Eden from his Trattato di architettura (1461–1464). It shows how Adam's arms sheltering his head is the source of the gable ended roof or pediment.*

Vitruuio
Adam

ground—or horizontal—plane to the vertical wall. [Fig. 3-17] Cornices, like the head, articulate the transition from the wall to the roof, from the vertical to horizontal or angular plane, and to the sky. [Fig. 3-18]

The Romans added to the repertoire of anthropomorphic forms by incorporating the *dome* as an important element in their architecture. Seeming immeasurable, it is a symbol of the cosmos. Prehistoric humans painted the walls and ceilings of caves with images that illustrated their interpretation of the cosmos and of their place in the world around them. [Fig. 3-19] The dome may represent a transformation of such caves into a formalized and constructed interior space—whether at the Pantheon in Rome or the Hall of the People at the Capitol in Washington D.C. The former articulates the world of the Roman Empire and the gods of its numerous peoples; the latter tells the story of the creation of the American republic through paintings on the walls. [Figs. 3-20a and b] In these contexts, the dome may also be seen as a metaphorical image of the human head and brain, the location of our collective memory.

Architectural historian David Summers tells us that, for the Renaissance architect, "the order of the human body is the most complex in creation, mirroring the world itself."[21] Through studies of the human body and of nature, ancient Greek, Roman, and Renaissance artists and scholars sought to deduce natural proportions and to codify those observations for use in architecture. Michelangelo wrote, "It is certain that architectural members depend on the members of man. Who has not been or is not a good mas-

ter of the human body, and most of all of anatomy, cannot understand anything of it."[22] According to Summers, Michelangelo believed that a "building is . . . a human organism and, more than that, a living human organism."[23]

Renaissance artists and architects believed that the human form was the apex of God's creation and embodied all the secrets of nature's ordered beauty. Through the process of measurement, architects sought to establish an ideal model of proportions based on the human body. Such a norm, they believed, would allow architecture to participate in and express divine order and the harmonies of creation.[24]

Anthropomorphism is the very core of classical architecture. It is the key to relating architecture to individual human beings. In addition to conveying the anatomical metaphor, it is crucial in relating the scale of buildings to the people who use or observe them and to relating buildings to their neighborhood context.

HUMAN SCALE

One of the important considerations in our anthropomorphic conception of buildings is that of *scale*. We assess the scale, or relative size, of a building by measuring it against the size of our own bodies. Thus we describe a structure as having a "human" or an "inhuman" scale; for example, an unusually large entrance may be "over" scaled. [Fig. 3-21a and b] A skyscraper, however, like New York's 790-foot high Woolworth Building (1913), at one time the tallest

LEFT
FIG. 3-17 *Plinth at the National Gallery (1941), Washington, D.C., designed by John Russell Pope.*

FACING PAGE
FIG. 3-18 *Proto-Corinthian capitals at Dupont Hall (2002), University of Delaware, Newark, Delaware, designed by the Author.*

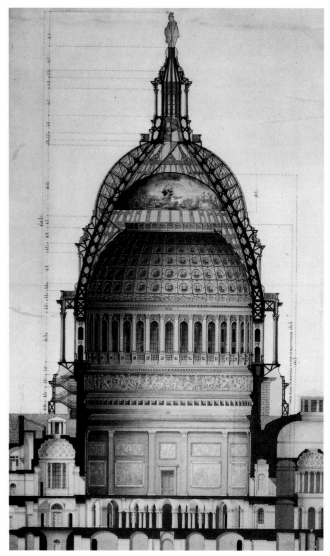

ABOVE LEFT
FIG. 3-19 *Interior view of the prehistoric Great Hall of the Bulls (15,000–10,000 B.C.), Lascaux II Grotto, Montignac, France.*

LEFT
FIG. 3-20a *Thomas U. Walter's rendering of the Hall of the People under his design for the new Capitol dome (1859).*

RIGHT
FIG. 3-20b *U.S. Capitol Rotunda, Washington, D.C., (1818–1866).*

building in the world, can be human in scale by virtue of the articulation of its façade, which assists an observer's eye and mind to measure it progressively, in parts, each of which is scaled to relate to a human being. [Figs. 3-22a, b, and c]

Consideration of a building's scale leads directly to the idea of *monumentality*. According to the English architectural historian Sir John Summerson, "Monumental architecture begins with the temple. The temple is a building of more-than-human scale, built to house a more-than-human personage—a god."[25] The key word in this definition is "*than*." In mathematics, "than" implies a ratio, a measurable relationship. Thus monumentality is the deliberate and measurable adjustment of a building's scale "beyond ordinary human needs in order to express the idea of something greater than humanity."[26] For example, to one standing in the nave of a Gothic cathedral the vertical thrust of the tall piers suggests immeasurability. The façade of Wells Cathedral (1180–1425) in England has stacked larger-than-life figures of the saints in the corner piers of the towers, which literally express the greater-than-human dedication of the cathedral. [Fig. 3-24]

ABOVE
FIG. 3-21a *Detail of the entrance of the IBM building (1961), New York, New York, designed by Edward L. Barnes.*

RIGHT
FIG. 3-21b *1400 I Street (1984), Washington, D.C., designed by Arthur Cotton Moore. The six-story-high recess shelters entrances to the building and to a metro station.*

FACING PAGE LEFT
FIG. 3-22a *Woolworth Building (1913), New York, New York, designed by Cass Gilbert.*

FACING PAGE RIGHT
FIG. 3-22b *Façade analysis of the Woolworth Building.*

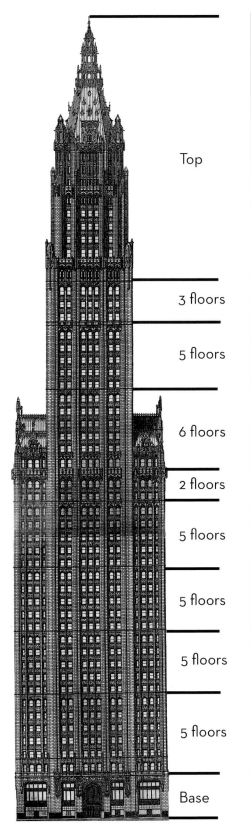

Top

3 floors

5 floors

6 floors

2 floors

5 floors

5 floors

5 floors

5 floors

Base

FIG. 3-22c *Detail of the façade of the Woolworth Building.*

FIG. 3-23 *West façade of Wells Cathedral (1180–1425), Somerset, England.*

A MODEST MONUMENTALITY
FOR A SECULAR DEMOCRACY

The Puritans forcefully rejected the monumental approach to architecture. They discarded the idea of the divine right of kings, of a theocracy of priests standing between them and their God, and of consecrating buildings. The implications for architecture were manifested in their meetinghouses. Designed as a larger version of a modest New England dwelling, the meetinghouse was an unconsecrated space that also served the community's secular needs as a venue for town meetings, court sessions, and school classes. [Fig. 3-24] That approach to architecture avoided the notion of monumentality expressed at Wells Cathedral. It would be unthinkable to use the nave of the cathedral for a public hearing on the town's budget. The Puritans' ideas about government, and of the architectural significance of the house as the basis of government buildings, remain fundamentally important to our democracy.

After the revolution, the architecture of some public buildings continued to develop the legacy of the Puritan ethos. The Maryland Statehouse is an eloquent example. The architecture explicitly suggests a home for the extended family that constitutes the people of the state. A large building, it has a domestic air that projects an unusual aura of architectural modesty. I call this attribute a *qualified* or *modest monumentality*. It is an important component of the architecture of democratic institutions because it makes citizens feel welcome in their statehouse—the home of all the citizens of the state. The house metaphor is an acknowledgment of the importance of the mundane, of the family- and work-related routines of everyday life. Therefore, the quality of modest monumentality is an expression of the dignity of labor and human

FIG. 3-24 *Meetinghouse (1770), Germantown, Pennsylvania.*

enterprise. Herman Melville exults in it in Moby Dick, when he speculates that the "august dignity I treat of, is not the dignity of kings and robes" for "thou shalt see it shining in the arm that wields a pick or drives a spike." It is "that great democratic dignity which, on all hands, radiates without end from God."[28] Melville also celebrates the "great democratic God" who selects "champions from the kingly commons," from ordinary people.[28] Melville celebrates the "just Spirit of Equality, which has spread one royal mantle of humanity over all my kind."[29]

By clearly expressing in our architecture that "We, the People," are the government of the United States, it is possible to transcend the vain aggrandizement of presidents, politicians, and civil servants. To do so secures a secular realm in which citizens—the true government—can feel comfortable. And because modesty is important in architecture as well as democratic government, a qualified monumentality should facilitate—to the extent architecture can—reasoned debate, respect for different points of view, and the need to balance conflicting spheres. Such a qualified form of monumentality is the reason that an important government building in a democracy might be smaller than the buildings around it.

The arrogance that was associated with the claims of the monarchy to a special relationship to the divine inhibits the search for truth. In public buildings it discourages the active participation of citizens who may feel unwelcome or intimidated. Arrogance undermines democracy in insidious ways. It suggests that leaders rule by right, with an entitlement to prevail and to impose their will. Summerson specifically warns against the temptation of borrowing "the attributes of God."[29] Kings believed they were more than ordinary human beings. Such pretensions in public office and in architecture would undermine the Constitution and subvert the principles of democracy.

MONUMENTALITY AND ARCHITECTURAL HUBRIS

In Europe, from the middle of the seventeenth century on, the word "monumental" was also used, more loosely, to describe colossal structures. Monumentality in that context was defined by absolute size and, as a result, any scale of reference related to an individual or to a person's *house* was jettisoned. Public buildings conceived between 1933 and 1945 by the Nazis in Germany provide an apt contemporary illustration of the role of absolute size in architecture.

Hitler's government buildings were gargantuan. Denied any possibility of a comparison to human scale, the visitor was overwhelmed. The quintessential example of this aggressive aesthetic is the unrealized plan for the Nazi Party's Grosse Halle (1937) in Berlin. It was designed by Hitler and his preferred architect, Albert Speer, as the focal point of a vast plan to reconstruct the capital city. [Fig. 3-25] A single domed space designed to hold 180,000 people, the Grosse Halle was intended to be nearly 1,000 feet high, significantly taller than the 525-foot-high Seagram Building (1958) on Park Avenue and the 790-foot-high Woolworth Building (1913) on lower Broadway, both in New York. In fact,

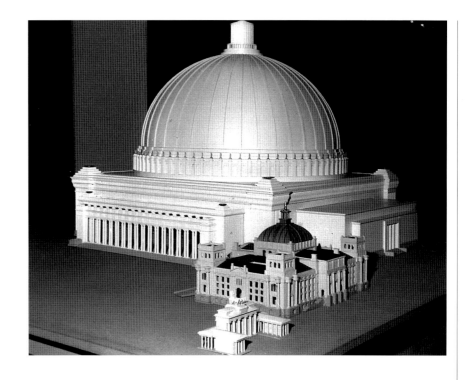

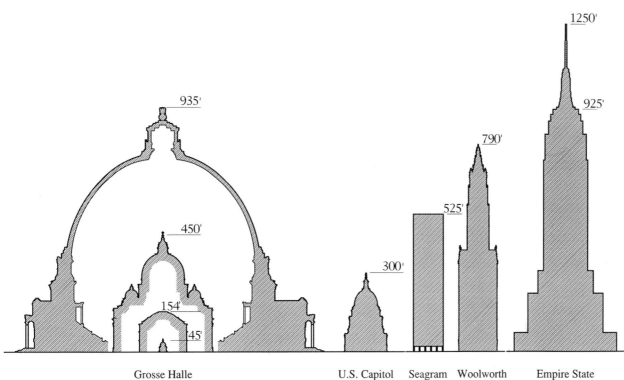

935'

1250'

925'

790'

525'

450'

300'

154'

45'

Grosse Halle
St. Peter's
Pantheon
Tempietto

U.S. Capitol   Seagram   Woolworth   Empire State

FIG. 3-25 *The Albert Speer and Adolf Hitler project to rebuild Berlin (1939).*

FIG. 3-26 *A comparative study of building sections drawn to the same scale. Reading from left to right: Grosse Halle (1937), St. Peter's in Rome, ancient Roman Pantheon, U.S. Capitol in Washington, D.C., and the Seagram Building (1958), Woolworth Building (1913), and Empire State Building (1931).*

FIG. 3-27 *A detail of the model of the Grosse Halle (1941), in Berlin, designed by Albert Speer and Adolf Hitler.*

its 154-foot-diameter lantern was so large that the 138-foot-diameter dome of St. Peters could pass through it. [Fig. 3-26]

The purpose of such grandiosity was to glorify Hitler and the regime that he created as an extension of his personality. Hitler wanted to overwhelm his visitors, his henchmen, and his fellow Germans, and, through the architectural setting, instill in them a sense of their own insignificance in his presence. Speer described his goal as:

> impos[ing] the grandeur of the building upon the people who are in it. If people who may have different minds are pressed together in such surroundings, they all get unified to one mind.[30]

In the Nazi cosmos, human beings were no longer made in the image of God and dedicated to the pursuit of truth and justice; they merely served the Fuhrer.

The scale of building Hitler chose for central Berlin presented a new relationship between architectural detail and building mass. Rather than muting the scale of a building's vast mass by breaking it up into smaller units, Hitler and Speer emphasized its absolute size. The Grosse Halle would have been so large that any connection to anthropomorphism would have been jettisoned; it was the embodiment of a cosmos with Hitler at its center. Its crudely formed entablature-like feature was to have been about 38-feet high—as large as a three-story building. [Fig. 3-27] At that scale, the balance of ornament, architectural elements, and anthropomorphic scale that is a fundamental characteristic of classical design becomes incoherent.

But anthropomorphic harmony was a quality Hitler disdained. He needed to employ extravagant scale and gargantuan size to distance his work from the architecture of the past and as a means of intimidation. In his study, *The Ghosts of Berlin*, Brian Ladd notes that the "idea that buildings represented traditions worth appropriating was foreign to [Hitler]. He had no desire to emulate those leaders in Moscow or Prague who took over royal residences."[31] For Hitler, the past was less than irrelevant. His desire was not merely to replace tradition; he was determined to obliterate it. This is true even though he used a dome, square columns, and a cornicelike feature at the top of the walls of the Grosse Halle. His forms are so much larger and so specifically anti-anthropomorphic and antihuman. There is none of the careful calibration of scale and sensuousness of form found in the classical language of architecture. Hitler's goal of obliterating the past mandated the creation of an architecture that could be used to build new cities and towns that would be a reflection of the goals of the society the Nazis were creating—a society worthy of the Aryan Reich—and a celebration of the triumph of national Socialism. [Fig. 3-28]

In this architectural endeavor, he actually followed in the footsteps of the early modernist architects of the 1920s. They dreamed of using new vocabularies of architectural form and city planning to replace Europe's old cities with modern ones that would reflect their particular visions of a new socialist utopia.[32] Modernists considered architectural antecedents obsolete.

The most influential modernist formulation of this aspiration was Le Corbusier's 1925 project for *Une Ville Contemporaine pour 3 Millions d'Habitants*. [Figs. 3-29a and b] It formed the basis of the 1925 *Plan "Voisin" de Paris*. [Figs. 3-29c and d] In it, Le Corbusier proposed demolition of a large L-shaped area on the right bank of the Seine River in Paris. He proposed to build in that area a group of eighteen cruciform skyscrapers, sixty stories high. Planned on a cross-axial grid, each would be about nine hundred feet tall. Between these towers, Le Corbusier proposed a network of highways set high above the ground on columns. The ground plane was to be a large park in which a few landmarks—the Place de la Concord, the Louvre, and Ile de la Cité—would be preserved. Residential buildings, about six stories high, formed the perimeter of the new Paris. The plan, like Hitler's project for Berlin a decade later, leaves a large part of the existing city intact; but in both cases, the design was the first step in the eventual obliteration of most of the old city.

FIG. 3-28 *The main axis of the model of Speer's and Hitler's project to rebuild Berlin (1939).*

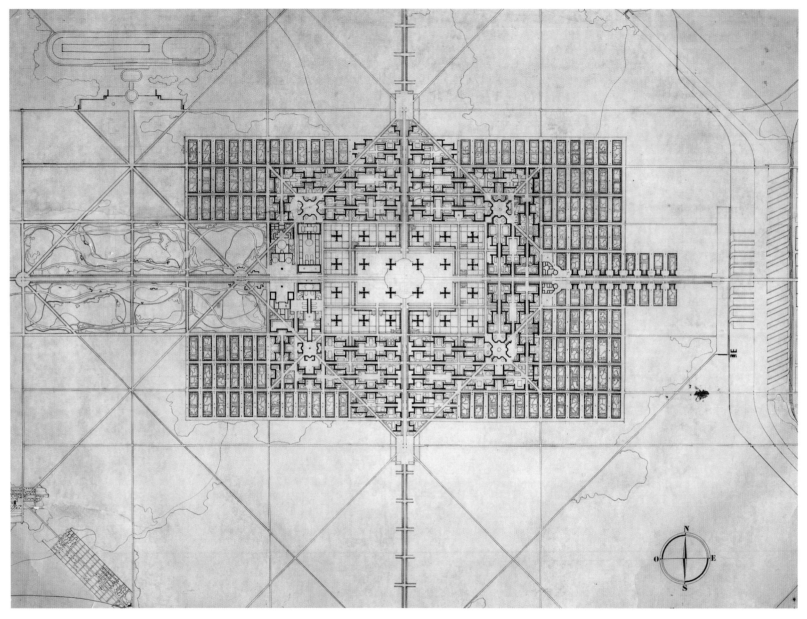

FIGS. 3-29a and b *Le Corbusier's plan* (ABOVE) *and perspective study* (BELOW) *of a* Ville de 3 millions d'habitants *(1925).*

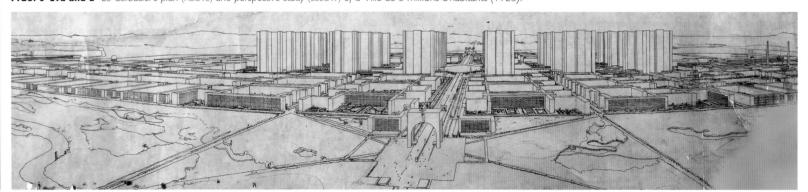

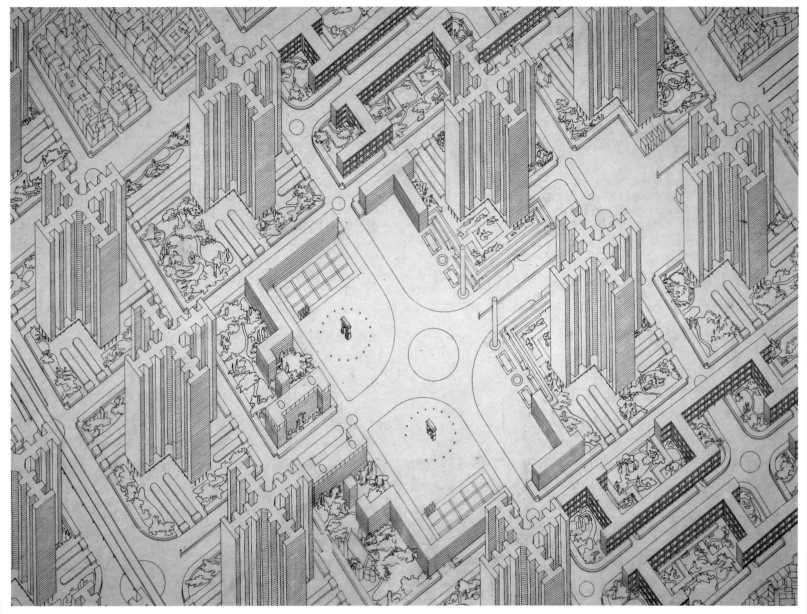

FIGS. 3-29c and d *Le Corbusier's perspective study* (ABOVE) *and axonometric study* (BELOW) *of the* Plan Voisin de Paris *(1925).*

Although those plans for Paris and Berlin are very different in character, they share common features: cross-axial plans related to extensive transportation facilities; nine-hundred-foot-high buildings that dwarf the scale of the old city—plans that can only be realized by a powerful, centralized form of government. Le Corbusier's plans were extremely influential. In fact, they probably influenced Speer's ideas for Berlin and certainly inspired the design of housing projects throughout the United States.[33] [Fig. 3-30] Le Corbusier and Hitler designed their versions of Paris and Berlin to celebrate the application of industrial technology and the new social and economic organization of their different forms of socialist utopia. It is important to note that that technology was already commonplace in the American building industry. That is why until the 1950s, there was no reason to feel a need to change the character of American architecture in order to express some desired relationship to industrial production. It is also why modernism in the United States was an aesthetic movement rather one related to social or political change.

Both of those city plans are for socialist societies in which the needs of individuals and families are fulfilled by an all-powerful government. They describe a relationship between the individual citizen and the government that is profoundly different from the democracy described in the Constitution of the United States. In their perceptive study, *Architects of Annihilation, Auschwitz and the Logic of Destruction*, Götz Aly and Susanne Heim describe "abandonment of moral restraint" as one of the three forces that animated the "executive dynamism of National Socialist Germany."[34] Hitler's drive to gargantuan scale may have been, in large part, related to his rejection of the necessity of "moral restraint." In this regard the complete dependence of individuals and families on the beneficence of the state is the most disturbing quality of the plans for Berlin—and Paris.

FIG. 3-31a *Empire State Building (1929–1931), New York, New York, designed by Shreve, Lamb and Harmon.*

TOP LEFT
FIG. 3-31b *View of Empire State Building from the Fifth Avenue sidewalk.*

BOTTOM LEFT
FIG. 3-32 *Annie Reed (Meg Ryan) meeting Sam Baldwin (Tom Hanks) and Johan Baldwin (Ross Malinger) on the observation deck of the Empire State Building from the movie* Sleepless in Seattle *(1993).*

A very different approach to monumental building in older and smaller-scaled neighborhoods is visible in the Empire State Building (1929–1931). [Fig. 3-31a] Although taller than the proposed Grosse Halle—it is 1,224 feet high at its topmost, 102nd story and 1,454 feet high if one includes the radio tower—the Empire State Building embodies a very different architectural philosophy. The lowest portion of the building, which defines the sidewalk, is only five floors high and effectively relates to the older buildings in the neighborhood. Next, a series of setbacks rise to relate to the height of successive generations of taller surrounding buildings. In a brilliant move, the shaft of the tower is set back from the busy Fifth Avenue sidewalk so that its great height does not loom over the pedestrians and make them feel insignificant. [Fig. 3-31b] In fact, the base of the shaft is not even visible from the adjacent sidewalks. On the narrower side streets, the tower setback is reduced, enhancing the drama experienced by pedestrians. Its anthropocentric focus may explain, in part, why this brilliant work of architecture remains the enduring symbol of New York, and why lovers in movies chose to meet on its observation deck even though there are now taller and newer buildings.[35] [Fig. 3-32]

A loss of anthropomorphic scale in architecture in general is not only due to factors related to the sheer size of buildings; it also implies a specific architectural decision to impose an unrelated and brutal design on an existing city or neighborhood. Such a decision is made by the client and the architect, and usually requires endorsement by the city government. An abandonment of anthropomorphic scale is the result of a drive to violate the complexity of what exists and to replace it with a new, more simplistic set of ideals and related architectural forms.

The Empire State Building's eloquent relationship to the pedestrians on the sidewalks of New York demonstrates the dynamic balance of anthropocentrism and skyscraper architecture that is possible in a democratic society. Sadly, that balance is lost in most new skyscrapers, which are freestanding, not only emphasizing their ostentatious height but also their disdain for the existing neighborhood. Even under King George III, in colonial Rhode Island, the reasoned harmony between the large Colony House—the seat of the Civil Court, Chamber of Deputies, and Council Room—and the surrounding city of Newport illustrates an architecture that embraced humanism. [Fig. 3-33]

FIG. 3-33 *Colony House (1739), Newport, Rhode Island.*

CONTEXTUALISM

If modest monumentality is one imperative of anthropomorphism in architecture, *contextualism* is the second. Contextual architecture is that which relates a building to its surrounding neighborhood. The nature of the relationship may be expressed in a fluid continuity of form, scale, and style, or in a more daring and calculated use of contrast. [Figs. 3-34a and b]. The choice depends upon the nature and significance of the institution housed in the building and its relationship to the community.

It is fair to ask why contextualism has a special relevance in a democratic society. Under the Constitution, the individual is the fundamental unit of the government; by extension, the anthropomorphic view of buildings and parts of buildings as metaphors for human anatomy may expand to encompass groups of buildings and even whole neighborhoods and the city. Thus a group, or community, of buildings is akin to a family or another community of people, a metaphor for the political structure by which citizens are related to each other and to a neighborhood, a city, a state, and, ultimately, a nation.

In *The Republic*, written in the fifth century BC, Plato asserted that different political and legal structures correspond to different types of human beings. He suggested that there is a direct correspondence between demo-cratic governments and their citizens, that men and women in a democracy are the cause and the effect of the democracy in which they are engaged.[36] Baron Montesquieu revived this idea in *Spirit of the Laws*, a book widely read by the generation of the founders. Architectural historian Carroll William Westfall also echoed Plato when he stated that "a public building is like a citizen . . . to see the individual . . . look at the city or state of which he is a citizen, since the state is man writ large and the individual is a microcosm of the state." Anthropomorphism is the central metaphor of the classical tradition, of its political philosophy, of its architecture, and of its city planning. That is why Westfall asserted that "anthropomorphism allows a building to represent the best of humankind. . . . It has always done this, and it has never repeated the way it has done this."[37]

Using ideas from both antiquity and Christian thought, Francesco di Giorgio, an important Italian Renaissance architect and the author of treatises on architecture and fortifications, expanded the search for a congruence of architectural form and the human body to the city. He proposed that "as the [human] body has all its members proportioned and subdivided according to perfect measure, so in the composition of temples, [and] the city . . . ought this to be observed." [Fig. 3-35] Such congruence underscores the concordat among American citizens to accept the founding documents as the basis of all

FIG. 3-34a *Church (1840), townhouse (1787), and schoolhouse (1884) in Washington, New Hampshire.*

FIG. 3-34b *View of New York c. 1870s.*

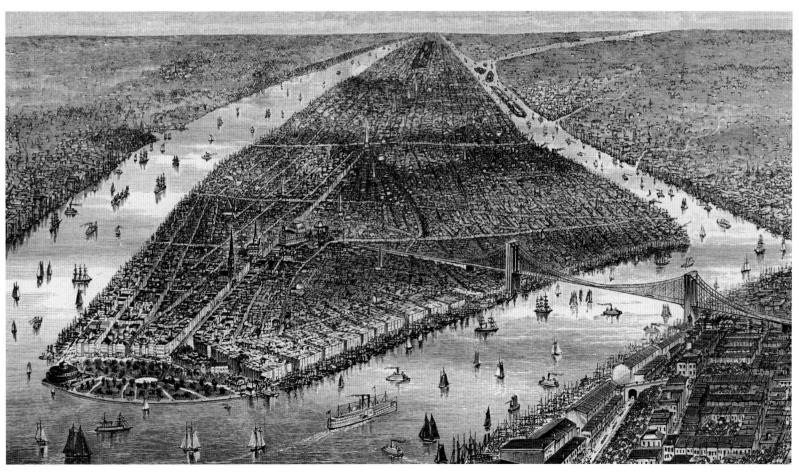

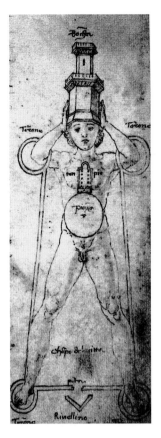

LEFT
FIG. 3-35 *Francesco di Giorgio, anthropomorphic image of the city from* Architettura, ingegneria. e arte militare *(c. 1476–1501).*

RIGHT
FIG. 3-36 *Schoolhouse (1850), Rome, Georgia.*

FACING PAGE
FIG. 3-37 *E. H. Suydam, "A Group of Lefcourt Buildings" (1929), illustrates office buildings in New York owned by the Lefcourt Corporation.*

laws; as a guide governing the relations between citizens, and as the basis for the conduct in business and political life. In addition, it reinforces the communitarian ideals that are an integral part of the idea of urbanism. That is especially important in a democracy, in which there is a more diffuse distribution of authority, wealth, and land ownership, and individual property owners exercise great autonomy in conducting their affairs.

Public buildings are not monuments to the elected and appointed officials who work in them, or to their architects. Rather, in Justice Wilson's words, public buildings in a democracy should reflect "the majesty of the people." The projection of civic authority should rely on variation of architectural scale through the notion of a modest monumentality. The ideas around which a public building is designed should be congruent with the ideals of the founding documents and, appropriately, celebrate the convenience of the citizenry— that is, of the government. [Fig. 3-36] If that does not occur, the social and political ends that the building is supposed to serve are undermined. A public building that ignores its neighborhood may also suggest that the people who live and work there, as well as the citizens whom the agencies in the building serve, were irrelevant or at best minor considerations to the client and architect. Lack of sensitivity to a building's surroundings may also suggest a lack of skill—or a measure of arrogance—in the architect.

In the powerful commercial context of pre-1930 lower Manhattan, one finds a revolutionary way of relating buildings to each other. At the turn of the twentieth century, competing corporate and real estate interests vied there to devise taller and taller buildings—skyscrapers. [Fig. 3-37] In 1914 a writer in the New York Tribune observed that "'Skyward, Ho' not 'Westward, Ho' is the cry of the capitalist."[38] Although there were few controls governing the scope of each building—no limits on floor area, height, and site coverage until the 1916 zoning regulation that related the height of a building to the width of the street—and no aesthetic controls or review process, this corporate jousting for attention, height, and identity created the unique skyline just north of Battery Park. It became the symbol of New York City, of America's technological preeminence and audacious courage, and of the twentieth century itself. Those buildings were constructed despite theories that they would cause Manhattan to sink in the mud and would increase the incidence of malaria and tuberculosis in the city.[39]

How can we account for such a successful experiment in city planning and architecture? The key factor appears to be the use of a common conceptual structure as the basis for the design: a pyramidal form of skyscraper comprising three different parts.[40] The first part is a base section that articulates the pedestrian's experience by providing visually interesting architecture that is

FIG. 3-38 *Cable Building (1892), New York, New York, designed by McKim, Mead and White.*

FIG. 3-39 *View of Lower Manhattan from Brooklyn, New York in 2004.*

usually two or three floors high. Designed to acknowledge the cone of vision and the scale of a person on the adjacent sidewalk, the base section is typically differentiated from the structure above—like the base molding that caps the foundation wall of a house. The second is an intermediate section that is formed by a tall shaft, usually articulated by setbacks, which reduce its mass as it soars skyward. Meant to be seen from farther away, its design is sculpturally more dynamic and its decorative detail is simple and repetitive. The third, top section is whimsical and usually pyramidal in form. Barely visible from the surrounding sidewalks, it was designed to contribute to the drama of the skyline. [Fig. 3-38]

In lower Manhattan, dozens of architects used very different styles, colors, and materials to design the boldly formed towers that vied for attention from the street and the horizon. But the key to the creation of this justly famous sky-

LEFT
FIG. 3-40 *Chase Manhattan Bank (1961), New York, New York, designed by Skidmore, Owings and Merrill.*

FACING PAGE
FIG. 3-41 *Lever House (1952), Park Avenue, New York, New York, designed by Skidmore, Owings and Merrill.*

FIG. 3-42 *View of the Chicago skyline in 2001.*

line was the general acceptance of the three-segment building as a common architectural concept—with all its formal implications—by owners, architects, and civil authorities. It was the basis of the design of all their very different buildings. In that sense it is a masterpiece of conceptual art. Sadly, this amazing collective work of art has been undermined by architectural hubris, which took the form of a new generation of taller, bulkier, boxlike buildings that share little beyond their larger floor plates, freestanding form, and vacant gaze. [Fig. 3-39] From their inception, such commercial buildings lacked even a glimmer of recognition of the urban character of lower Manhattan; in fact, their designers generally failed to acknowledge the older conceptual paradigm of the area. That is clearly evident in the Chase Manhattan Bank building (1961) designed by Skidmore, Owings and Merrill, which was inspired by their earlier Lever House (1952). [Figs. 3-40 and 3-41] Following the example of New York, the skylines of cities around the globe are now formed by similar but unrelated boxlike, self-referential buildings. [Fig. 3-42]

The architectural generation that created New York's skyline in the nineteenth and early twentieth centuries also integrated new building types such as large department stores, apartment buildings, schools, great bridges, and even power plants into existing urban environments. [Figs. 3-43 and 3-44] Inventive design, contrast of scale, and a common vocabulary of form—usually, but not always, classical—were essential to the integration of these large structures into the urban landscape. In the case of bridges, all three ingredients were essential. That is clearly demonstrated at the Manhattan Bridge (1909), designed by architects Carrère and Hastings and engineers Foster Nichols and Leon Moisseiff. An unusual colonnade frames the roadway's transition onto the

FIG. 3-43 *View of the recently constructed Manhattan Bridge (1909) from a street in New York.*

FIG. 3-44 *Consolidated Edison's Waterside Generating Station (1905) at 40th Street and First Avenue, New York, New York.*

FOLLOWING PAGES
FIG. 3-45 *Aerial view of the entrance to the Manhattan Bridge from Manhattan, New York.*

bridge. [Fig. 3-45] The huge mass of the bridge's abutment is integrated into the surroundings by powerfully sculpted forms that convey a sense of the tensile stresses of the suspension cables as well as the resisting compressive force of the masonry. [Figs. 3-46a and b] The large and primary forms of the classical moldings and details, in both metal and stone, are key elements relating the contrasting scale of the adjacent city. Variations of these same architectural forms, albeit at a much smaller scale, animate the design of residential and commercial buildings as well as household furniture and silver. [Figs. 3-47a, b, and c] This is possible because the classical design vocabulary is sufficiently comprehensive to include everything in its family of forms, from salt shakers to furniture, to buildings, bridges, and cities.

Contextual architecture in a democratic capitalist society relies on three very different commitments. The first is to a common responsibility for the neighborhood and for the city, which has to be shared among citizens, architects, clients, civic authorities, and developers. Although the colonial towns of the Puritans provided a dramatic example of contextual forces based on the use of common materials and similar architectural forms—often a product of necessity—it was the architecture of their meetinghouses that illustrated their communitarian commitment. The architectural expression of this responsibility can be seen in the wide acceptance of a common vocabulary of form in the towns of eighteenth-century New England and early-nineteenth-century America. [Fig.3-48]

The second commitment is to the reconfiguration of the scale of public buildings from the majestic European model to structures of modest monumentality. The initial steps in that direction were taken by the Puritans and Mennonites when they designed both their meetinghouses—the most important buildings in their communities—and their town houses as larger versions of local houses. A similar reconfiguration is also evident in the federal design of the Massachusetts State House, which dominated the early nineteenth-century skyline of Boston. Its tall, gold dome was the first structure on the horizon visible to ships sailing into the harbor. [Fig. 3-49] That contrast occurs in reverse at the New York City Hall; today, it is much smaller than the surrounding structures. [Fig. 3-50]

The third necessary commitment is to the use of the same conceptual paradigm for most buildings in a neighborhood. [Fig. 3-51] Acceptance of a common aesthetic allows for the wide range of stylistic variation we see in lower Manhattan, a vocabulary that includes the gothic Woolworth Building and the classical form of the Standard Oil Building (1922).

LEFT
FIG. 3-46a *Abutment of the Manhattan Bridge.*

FACING PAGE
FIG. 3-46b *A pier of the Manhattan Bridge.*

ABOVE

FIG. 3-47a *Huguenot silver sugar and spice casters (1728), made in London and brought to North America.*

RIGHT

FIG. 3-47b *Sterling silver candlesticks (c. 1790), Philadelphia, made by Joseph Richardson, Jr.*

BELOW

FIG. 3-47C *A knee-hole desk (1770–1785), Newport, Rhode Island, made by Daniel Goddard.*

FIG. 3-48 *First Ohio Statehouse (1803), Chillicothe, Ohio.*

FELCH—RICHES.

FIG. 3-49 Boston Harbor (1856) painted by Fitz Hugh Lane. The dome of the Massachusetts Statehouse on Beacon Hill is visible in the distance.

FIG. 3-50 *The New York City Hall (1803–1811), New York, New York, designed by Joseph Francois Mangin and John McComb, Jr.*

FACING PAGE
FIG. 3-51 *Photograph of Lower Manhattan looking south from Chelsea.*

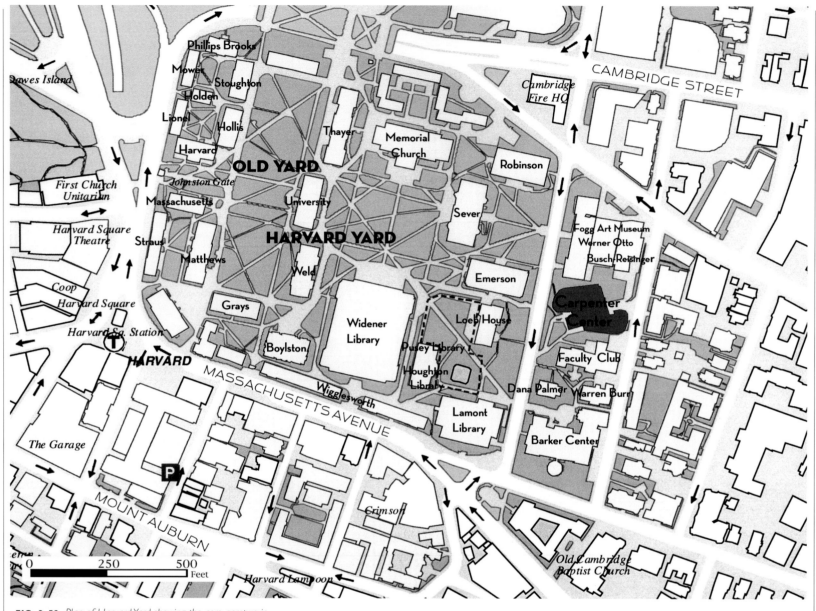

FIG. 3-52 *Plan of Harvard Yard showing the core campus in Cambridge, Massachusetts. Carpenter Center (1963) is highlighted.*

A CAREFULLY CALCULATED INVERSION

The most daring example of the application of these design ideas to create an exciting contextual harmony is Le Corbusier's Carpenter Center (1963) at Harvard University. Colonial, federal, and classical models inspired the older campus buildings. Rectangular in form, set parallel to the street and to other buildings in the Harvard Yard, those brick or wood structures formed the courtyards that characterized the campus. [Fig. 3-52] Disdaining a safe-

ty net, Le Corbusier ingeniously inserted an avant-garde structure into the rich fabric of the Yard. [Figs. 3-53a and b] He succeeded because he was able to draw upon a profound understanding of the history of architecture to create a set of architectural forms that invert, at precisely 180 degrees, the ideas on which the older surrounding buildings and the campus plan are based.

Like the surrounding buildings, Carpenter Center is cubic in form. Set at forty-five degrees to the street, its massing does not define the street or near-

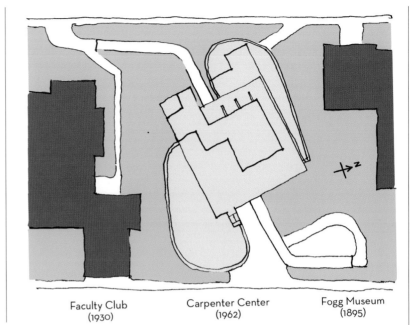

FIG. 3-53a *Detail plan of Carpenter Center and the adjacent Fogg Museum and Faculty Club.*

FIG. 3-53b *View of Carpenter Center (1963), designed by Le Corbusier, from across Quincy Street.*

Faculty Club
(1930)

Carpenter Center
(1962)

Fogg Museum
(1895)

FIG. 3-54 *View of the entrance ramp to Carpenter Center.*

FIG. 3-55 *Ramp moving through the fourth floor level at Carpenter Center.*

FIG. 3-56 *Piloti at Carpenter Center.*

by sidewalk. [Fig. 3-54] In a dramatic gesture, Le Corbusier swept the sidewalk up into the air and drove it through the fourth-floor level of the building, and then dropped it down to the adjacent street. [Fig. 3-55] Continuing to reverse normal expectations, Carpenter Center is not set on the ground; rather, it is raised up in the air as if weightless, supported on thin posts that Le Corbusier called *piloti*. [Fig. 3-56] Rather than siting the building in a garden of lawn and shrubs, Le Corbusier put the garden on the roof, on a series of terraces. [Fig. 3-57] Eschewing traditional load-bearing walls, Le Corbusier designed walls with long, ribbonlike windows that emphasized the apparent weightlessness of the building mass. He protected the art studios from direct sunlight and glare by building an independent, egg-crate–like concrete structure (he called it a

brise-soleil) in front of the glass. In that way he avoided using curtains or blinds. [Fig. 3-58] Finally, in a moving gesture of reconciliation and integration, Le Corbusier filled in the voids between his diagonal exterior walls and the adjacent orthogonal structures with soft, round, balloonlike forms that seem to float in the air despite the support of the long, thin piloti.

Unfortunately, like the skyline of lower Manhattan, the architectural authority of Carpenter Center has been undermined by the next generation of buildings. Ironically, those new buildings at Harvard were created by students of Le Corbusier who lacked his profound understanding of the architecture of the past. They failed to grasp that his design was totally dependent on a precisely calculated contrasting tension with older adjacent buildings.

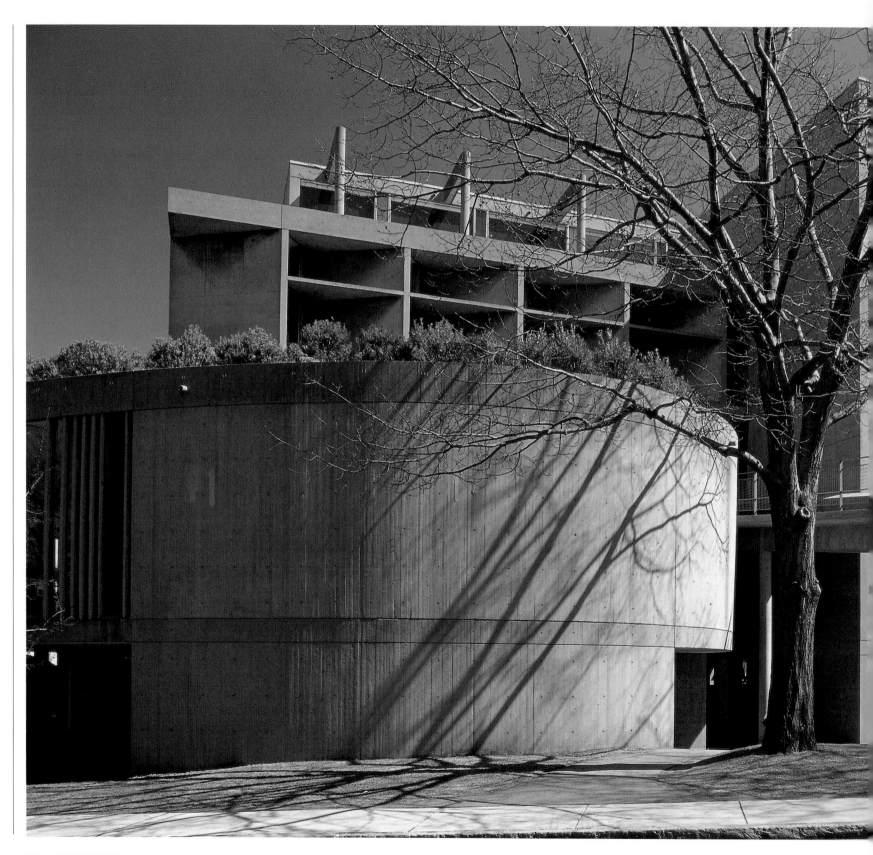

FIG. 3-57 *Roof garden at Carpenter Center.*

FIG. 3-58 *Brise Soleil at Carpenter Center.*

FIG. 3-59 *Graduate School of Design (1972), Harvard University, Cambridge, Massachusetts, designed by John Andrews.*

FIG. 3-60a *View of the poorly defined public space under an office building in Washington, D.C., that serves as the entrance to the building and to a metro station (1984).*

FACING PAGE
FIG. 3-60b *Science Center (1966–68), Harvard University, designed by Jose Luis Set, viewed through one of Harvard's beautiful gates.*

Maintaining that tension requires the older structures to be frozen in time so that they can continue to serve as the sounding board against which Le Corbusier's newer forms can resonate. Thus, by imitating Le Corbusier's work in the planning of his new Graduate School of Design (1972), John Andrews actually undermines the intensity of contrast between Carpenter Center and such older adjacent buildings as the Fogg Museum. [Fig. 3-59]

Andrews's building, like most other new buildings on the campus, disdains formal architectonic relationships with its neighbors. As new buildings grow in number and bulk, they are eroding the unique character of the campus. [Fig. 3-60a and b] Both Harvard's administration and its architects seem to eschew the notion of architectural continuity. They have forgotten Oscar Wilde's wry aphorism: "Nothing is so dangerous as being too modern. One is apt to grow old fashioned quite suddenly."[41]

Perhaps they consider the idea of using new buildings to maintain, even enhance, the integrity of the campus to be obsolete. Such a limited approach to architecture continues to dominate Harvard's new planning despite the palpable intelligence, courage, and character of the older campus, which continues to define Harvard's identity. Of the new buildings, only Carpenter Center, now more than four decades old, remains avant-garde.

No other twentieth-century modernist architect was as involved with the past or imbued his work with a more austere and Calvinist vision than Le Corbusier; that his work is so undermined at Harvard must roil the souls of John Calvin's Puritan disciples who founded the university in the seventeenth century as a stronghold of intellectual endeavor. The challenge of engaging Le Corbusier's masterpiece in its context at the edge of the Harvard Yard recalls T. S. Eliot's haunting lines:

And the end of all our exploring
Will be to arrive at where we started
And to know the place for the first time.[42]

The fate of lower Manhattan and Carpenter Center teaches us that simplistic concepts of architecture's role and responsibilities inevitably demean the quality of architecture and the surrounding environment. Writing about new architecture in Manhattan in 1962, the *New York Times* protested that "New York's builders are well on the way to turning the city into a bottomless—and topless—morass of mediocrity."[43] Such derelictions of intelligence have created what Norman Mailer poignantly characterized as the "empty landscapes of psychosis."[44] [Figs. 3-61a and b]

FIG. 3-61a *View looking north up Sixth Avenue, New York, at the new section of Rockefeller Center.*

FIG. 3-61b *View of the poorly defined public space under an office building in Washington, D.C., that serves as the entrance to the building and to a metro station (1984).*

FIG. 3-62 *An aerial view of Thomas Jefferson's Academical Village (1826), University of Virginia, Charlottesville, Virginia.*

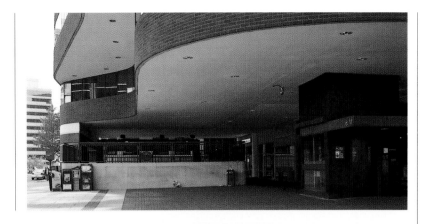

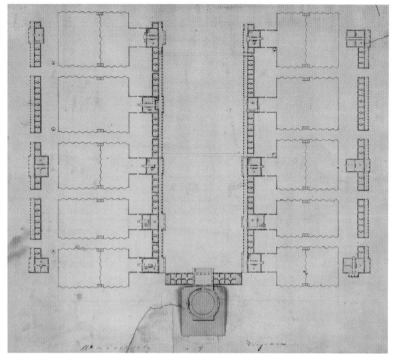

FIG. 3-63 *Plan of the Academical Village engraved by Peter Maverick in 1822.*

FIG. 3-64 *Upper Library (1693–1695) at Queens College, Oxford University, Oxford, England.*

Perhaps the most eloquent exemplar of the founders' vision of a new architecture for a democratic society is Jefferson's masterwork, the "academical village" of the University of Virginia. It is appropriate that a university is the nation's most accomplished work of architecture; both Jefferson and Washington recognized education as the cornerstone of a democracy. Washington died in 1799 and provided money in his will to endow a university in Washington, D.C. In 1786 Jefferson wrote from Paris to his old teacher, George Wythe, professor of law at the College of William and Mary, that "by far the most important bill in our whole code is that for the diffusion of knowledge among the people. No other sure foundation can be devised, for the preservation of freedom and happiness."[45] He devoted the last decade of his life to realizing an exemplary university not far from Monticello in Charlottesville, Virginia. To this end, he drafted the legislation, selected the site, lobbied the state legislature for funding, created the site plan, designed the buildings, searched for the best professors in each subject, and served as the first rector. It was to be more than a place parents sent children (sons only in Jefferson's time) for an education.[46] Jefferson referred to it as an "academical village," a community of scholars and students structured on the love of learn-

FIG. 3-65 *Tercentenary Yard at Harvard University.*

FOLLOWING PAGES
FIG. 3-66 *The Lawn, pavilions, colonnades, and rotunda at the University of Virginia as seen by a visitor arriving at the lower end of the campus in the nineteenth century.*

ing. And, unlike most universities prior to the revolution, it was a secular rather than religious institution. It served the interests of democracy by its dedication to the pursuit of truth and justice unfettered by considerations of theological dogma or political expediency. [Fig. 3-62]

JEFFERSON'S ACADEMICAL VILLAGE

All architecture proposes an effect on the human mind, not merely a service to the human frame. —JOHN RUSKIN *(The Seven Lamps of Architecture)*

The Academical Village forms the oldest part of the campus of the University of Virginia. Completed in 1826, Jefferson's design is based on an unusual idea: to erect a group of buildings planned in the form of a human being with arms open in a gesture of welcome. [Fig. 3-63] His architecture extends an invitation to a visitor to enter its grounds. In this respect it is very different from the cloistered colleges of Oxford University in England or even the more open courtyards of eighteenth-century Harvard. [Figs. 3-64 and 3-65]

The campus has four components, based on the metaphor of the human body. The first is the head—the library—a cylindrical building with a domed roof to shelter the books that serve as the university's brain; its pediment is the brow. Jefferson was inspired by the ancient Roman Pantheon, a building thought to have been a temple dedicated to the gods of the various nations in the empire. He deftly exploited this symbolism, together with the dome's association with the cosmos, to suggest that the library was a temple dedicated to the universe of knowledge. [Fig. 3-66]

FIG. 3-67 *Rotunda steps at the Academical Village. The metal railings are an unfortunate recent addition marring Jefferson's masterpiece.*

The next component is the structure's two 620-foot-long arms, one on each side of a landscaped terrace. Each arm is composed of five two-story pavilions connected by low colonnades. The pavilions have classrooms on the first floor and faculty apartments on the second. [Figs. 3-67 and 3-69] Each colonnade forms a covered walkway sheltering doors to a row of students' small rooms. The third and fourth components of the Academical Village are the shoulders of the composition, the two half-buried corridors connecting the library and colonnades, and the terrace between the arms, called the Lawn. The latter is divided into three terraces to accommodate a ten-foot change of grade. [Fig. 3-68]

At the rear of each pavilion is a garden surrounded by a serpentine wall, one for the use of each faculty apartment. [Fig. 3-70] Walkways between the walls connect the Lawn to the east and west ranges, a row of student rooms separated by three dining halls Jefferson called "hotels." [Fig. 3-71] Arcades

FIG. 3-68 *Terraces on the Lawn at the Academical Village.*

shelter a continuous walkway that extends across the façade of each range and defines the outer edge of the village. Because the site slopes from east to west, there is also an asymmetry in the size of the gardens on the east and west sides of the lawn.

A visitor enters the Academical Village from the open south end and walks up to the library rotunda; because Jefferson elected not to provide a path on the Lawn to the library, most people prefer to walk through the colonnades. He did build stairs between the three terraces to negotiate the changes of level. [Fig. 3-72]

The architecture of the campus is unusually complex. Jefferson juxtaposed buildings of different size—the large rotunda, smaller pavilions, and long, low colonnades—to create an arrangement of architectural forms and masses that enchants the eye with variety and captivates the mind with its metaphorical images of the human body. Jefferson went further by designing

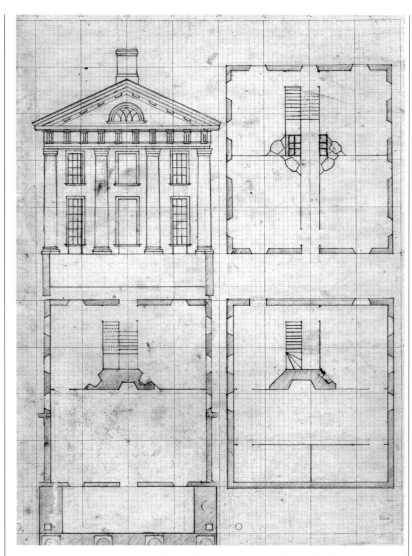

FIG. 3-69 *Elevation and plans of Pavilion IV at the Academical Village (1819).*

FIG. 3-70 *Serpentine Walls at the Academical Village.*

a completely different façade for each of the ten pavilions. That allowed him to exploit the tension between them and the near symmetry of the massing of the five pavilions on either side of the Lawn. [Figs. 3-73a and b] The façade of each pavilion is a variation on the theme of the ancient Roman temple using one- and two-story columns, brick arcades, and even a niche. There is no repetition, only a playful game, exploring forms and scale within the same thematic context.

Jefferson wrote to Dr. William Thornton, the winner of the competition for the new United States Capitol in Washington, D.C., that he wanted to use the façades of the pavilions as a way of teaching students about architecture: the "pavilions . . . will shew . . . a variety of appearance, no two alike, so as to serve as specimens for the architectural lectures." But, as we have noted, he also wanted to counter the insistent architectural focus on the library. The tension between the competing rhythms and juxtapositions of scale that animate each side of the Lawn are compelling enough to serve that purpose. Why did Jefferson go to all this trouble? Beyond illustrating ideas from architectural history and enriching the walk to the library, the campus design demonstrates an important lesson for students who will soon be active in the political life of a

FIG. 3-71 *Terraces on the Lawn at the Academical Village.*

great democracy: how to create sublime harmony out of differences, unity of purpose out of endless variety, and balance out of asymmetry.

Not yet satisfied, Jefferson introduced another level of design complexity by manipulating perspective. [Fig. 3-74] Within the apparently regular composition of pavilions and colonnades that defines each side of the Lawn, Jefferson carefully decreased the spacing between the pavilions by progressively reducing the number of student rooms between them as they approach the rotunda. The spacing does not decrease at the same rate on both sides—on the east side of the Lawn the number of rooms decreases from eight student

rooms to seven, to six, and to four; on the west side from ten rooms to seven, to six, and to four. This exquisite articulation intensifies the perspective by making the rotunda appear nearer than it actually is when seen from the entrance to the campus. The effect is made more palpable by an ingenious countertension. Jefferson increased the length of the three terraces in the rise on the Lawn between the entrance and the rotunda steps in direct opposition to the growing closeness of the pavilions. That countertension makes the rotunda appear farther away, causing the viewer's attention to oscillate between the architecture of the pavilions and colonnades and the strong visual emphasis on

FIG. 3-72 *Pavilion IX at the Academical Village.*

the library building. Jefferson used the architecture of the Academical Village to embody a second important lesson for students: that appearances are not always what they seem, and truth is often hidden by complex circumstances.

Jefferson's final touch was to separate the system of pathways, designed for circulation within the complex, from the system of axes, or lines of force, projected into space by the mass of the various buildings. [Figs. 3-75 and 3-76] The result is that the architecture is experienced from pathways obliquely, in angular and interesting compositions, rather than head-on, which would make the buildings appear more formal and more detached. In this context, it is important to remember that Jefferson did not provide a formal path up the center of the Lawn to conduct visitors to the library. That would have subdivided the Lawn and diminished the intensity of the conversation between the two rows of pavilions and colonnades. Adding formality to the complex of buildings would have undermined Jefferson's desire to use the Lawn to unify the campus and to provide a relaxed setting for quiet study and conversation as well as active student games.

FIG. 3-73a *Pavilion III at the Academical Village.*

FIG. 3-73b *Pavilions IV and VI at the Academical Village showing variations on the temple front design.*

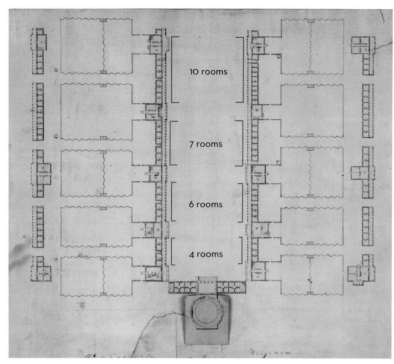

FIG. 3-74 *Plan of the Academical Village showing the variation in the number of student rooms between the pavilions.*

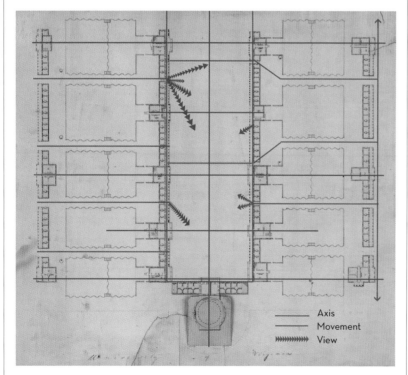

————	Axis
————	Movement
»»»»»»»	View

FIG. 3-75 *Building axes and walkways between pavilions.*

RIGHT **FIG. 3-76** *Pavilions seen from a cross-walkway entering the Colonnade.*

FIG. 3-77 *A "difficult joint" between a pavilion and the colonnade.*

FIG. 3-78 *Ecole Européenne de Chirurgie (1774), Paris, France, designed by Jacques Gondoin.*

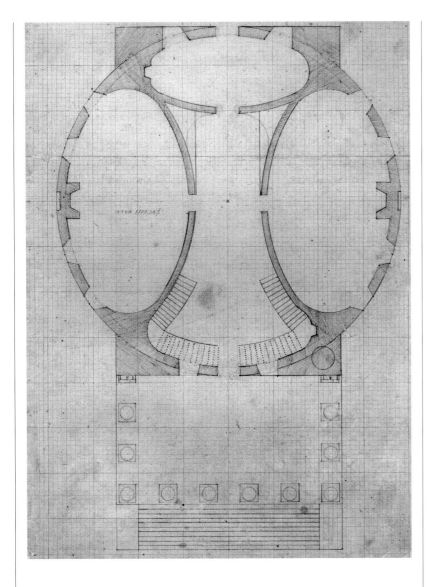

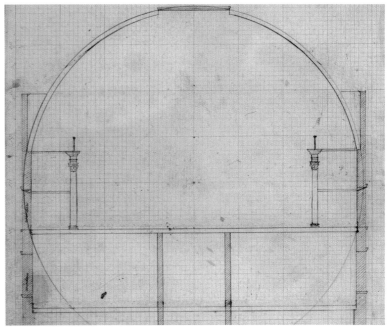

FIG. 3-79 *Plan of the lower level of the Rotunda (1821) of the Academical Village at the University of Virginia.*

FIG. 3-80 *A section through the Rotunda at the Academical Village.*

The most challenging aspect of Jefferson's relentless drive to create a fitting expression of American democracy in architecture may be the unique junctions he created between each pavilion and its adjacent colonnade. [Fig. 3-77] In some cases the colonnade continues across the front of the pavilion; in others it stops short. There are also places where pavilion and colonnade attempt to engage each other. Given that Jefferson was aware of how European architects resolved such problems—at Jacques Gondoin's Ecole de Chirurgie (1774) in Paris, for example [Fig. 3-78]—we cannot dismiss that decision as an example of architectural naiveté on the part of our greatest architect. He clearly chose to design those joints that way. Why? Because he wished to articulate, in physical, architectural form, the "difficult" passage of knowledge between students and professors. Like the complex joints of the human body that facilitate the transfer of energy to enable movement—like ankles, knees, and knuckles—Jefferson's junctions project a sense of the complicated process of learning and understanding between faculty and students.[47]

There is another difficult joint between the colonnade and the library. It involves a transition from the open colonnade, through a ninety-degree turn and change of level, down to a half-underground corridor to the library's ground floor. At this level the library has two elliptical-shaped rooms and a double stair to the main floor of the reading room above. [Fig. 3-79] The noble flight of steps from the Lawn up to the portico is an open invitation to enter into the domed interior and be initiated into the wondrous world of knowledge. Although the Roman Pantheon served as inspiration, it is very different from Jefferson's design for the library. The university's semicircular dome

springs from a point much nearer to the floor. [Fig. 3-80] Jefferson also created a screen of columns to define the two tiers of stacks for the books. Following the example of the Pantheon, he introduced an oculus at the top of the dome. [Fig. 3-81] That established a vertical axis around which the carrels of knowledge seem to orbit and marks the culmination of the composition.

Jefferson believed that public buildings should be "temples dedicated to the sovereignty of the people." The Academical Village is a temple complex dedicated to the search for knowledge and truth, and, as such, it is the noblest expression of Jefferson's hopes for the nation.[48] The creation of a self-taught architect, it is unlike any other complex of buildings in the United States. Its design sophistication rivals the Acropolis, another group of many buildings harmoniously related to each other and the surrounding landscape. Jefferson's Academical Village creates a coherent community; it is the apogee of architectural endeavor in the United States.

Although the academical village is revered as an architectural masterpiece, the nineteenth and early twentieth century campus buildings typically use a tepid Jeffersonian architectural vocabulary but ignore his ingenious plan. The vast new campus that developed after 1950 has, with very few exceptions, ignored all aspects of Jefferson's fecund design. These new buildings could be located almost anywhere in the world without seeming out of place. The University's stewardship of the campus failed to rise to the expectations latent in the spirit and the intelligence of the forms Jefferson lovingly created around the Lawn.

THE ARCHITECTURE OF DEMOCRACY

The American emphasis on unpretentiousness in architecture—in scale and materials used—is also evident in the simple and elegant line and sparing use of ornament in American furniture design. The description of American simplicity in furniture by noted antiques dealer Albert Sack also applies to most American architecture up to the 1930s. He writes that "ornament dominated English furniture masterpieces" while Americans seemed to prefer quality of line and proportion. [Fig. 3-82] Our finest craftsmen developed architectural and furniture forms with "skillful restraint to a degree unsurpassed in England or France in the eighteenth century."[49] [Fig. 3-83] Americans inverted the prevailing symbolism: rich ornament was a metaphor for royal authority; the emphasis on quality of line and proportion became a product of democracy. Although many of our best cabinetmakers, craftsmen, and architects were Englishmen who immigrated to America, they seemed to grasp immediately "the American spirit of simplicity" and capture it in their work. That was poignantly articulated by Jefferson's close friend and neighbor James Madison in *Federalist #14*:

> Is not the glory of the people of America that, whilst they have paid a decent regard to the opinion of former times and other nations, they have not suffered a blind veneration for antiquity, for custom, or for names, to overrule the suggestions of their own good sense, their knowledge of their own situation, and the lessons of their own experience?

FACING PAGE
FIG. 3-81 *Interior view of the Rotunda at the Academical Village as rebuilt in 1973 by the University of Virginia. This design, based on Jefferson's incomplete sketches, replaced the wonderful interior created by Stanford White of McKim, Mead, and White in 1898 after Jefferson's interior was destroyed by a fire in 1895.*

FIG. 3-82 *An American lowboy (c. 740–1780)*

FIG. 3-83 *An English carved mahogany "ribband" back chair (1760).*

NOTES

1. The Gettysburg Address and Second Inaugural have, respectively, 271 and 702 words.

2. The symbolism of the Mall is discussed in my book *George Washington, Architect* (London: Andreas Papadakis, 1999).

3. In my notes that are more than ten years old, I found the following phrase: "teach civility to citizens by having the visible form of its buildings present the ontological ideals of its citizens." I have misplaced the source and apologize to the author for the failure to properly acknowledge his or her contribution to my thought about the Mall. If anyone has this information, I would appreciate your sending it to me so that I may amend the omission in all subsequent editions.

4. Even a plea on Ms. Anderson's behalf by Eleanor Roosevelt was ignored by the Daughters of the American Revolution in whose building the concert hall was located. It should be noted that the DAR's behavior was not unusual at the time. They employed the same policy of racial segregation as many other concert venues in the United States at the time, including the Metropolitan Opera House in New York.

5. The memorial was the brainchild of Cleve Jones, a gay rights activist in San Francisco, who surely merits recognition as a great conceptual artist.

6. At the time, the library under the rotunda was designed by Stanford White. He had been commissioned to rebuild Jefferson's library after it was destroyed by fire in the late nineteenth century. In an act of vandalism, the university demolished White's magnificent interior and replaced it with a cheap approximation of Jefferson's design.

7. Jane Jacobs, *The Death and Life of Great American Cities* (New York: Random House, 1961).

8. Henry Hope Reed, *The Golden City* (Garden City, New York: Doubleday, 1959).

9. Vincent Scully, *The Earth, the Temples, and the Gods: Greek Sacred Architecture* (New Haven, Conn.: Yale University Press, 1962).

10. Colin Rowe, "The Mathematics of the Ideal Villa: Palladio and Le Corbusier Compared," later reprinted in Rower, *The Mathematics of the Ideal Villa & Other Essays* (Cambridge, Mass.: MIT Press, 1976), 1–29.

11. Alexis de Tocqueville, *Democracy in America* (Chicago: University of Chicago Press, 2000), 3.

PART I: THE AMERICAN HOUSE

1. *The Man Who Shot Liberty Valance*, 1962 (Ford Productions-Paramount), directed by John Ford, produced by Willis Goldbeck, script written by James Warner Bellah and Willis Goldbeck from a story by Dorothy M. Johnson.

2. King James I, "A Speech to the Lords and Commons of the Parliament at White-Hall, on Wednesday the XXI, of March, anno 1609."

3. Herman Melville, *Moby-Dick, or, the Whale* (New York: Modern Library, 2000), 166.

4. This was the result of the Magna Carta and of William the Conqueror's division of the countryside into noncontiguous aristocratic estates. (The Glorious Revolution of 1688 further limited the English king's prerogatives. I am indebted to Professor Carroll William Westfall for reminding me of the complex limits on royal authority in England.)

5. Mark Girouard, "The Power House," *The Treasure Houses of Britain, Five Hundred Years of Private Patronage and Art Collecting* (Washington D. C.: National Gallery of Art and New Haven and London: Yale University Press, 2005), 22–23.

6. Kenneth Clark, "The Smile of Reason," Program 10, *Civilization, A Personal View* (1969), A 13-Part Series for Television Produced by the British Broadcasting System. "The Smile of Reason," was directed by Michael Gill and the series was conceived, written, and narrated by Kenneth Clark. Quotations were transcribed by the author from a VHS copy of the program broadcast on television.

7. Kenneth Clark, "The Smile of Reason," *Civilization, A Personal View* (New York: Harper & Row, Publishers, 1969), 265.

8. Bernard Bailyn, "Politics and the Creative Imagination," To Begin the World Anew, the Genius and Ambiguities of the American Founders (New York: Alfred A. Knopf, 2003), 4.

9. Ibid., 32.

PART II: PUBLIC BUILDINGS

1. Alexis De Tocqueville, *Democracy in America*, vol. 1, part 1, ch. 4, concluding sentences.

2. Alan Gowans, *Images of American Living, Four Centuries of Architecture and Furniture as Cultural Expression* (New York: HarperCollins, 1976), 88.

3. Familiarity with the language of the Bible was part of a seventeenth-century university education for Catholics and Protestants in Europe and England. Such knowledge was also required in the new American Puritan colleges like Harvard and Yale, both of which also collected Hebrew texts.

4. Eugene R. Fingerhut, "Were the Massachusetts Puritans Hebraic?" *The New England Quarterly*, 40:4, (December 1967), 521.

5. *American Revision to Westminster Confession of Faith*, Appendix (1647). See also *London Baptist Confession of Faith*, 1689. This was based on the Westminster Confession of Faith, 1646, ch. 29.

6. Alan Gowans, *Images of American Living, Four Centuries of Architecture and Furniture as Cultural Expression* (New York: HarperCollins, 1976), 68.

7. Ibid., 63.

8. Marian Card Donnelley, *The New England Meeting Houses of the Seventeenth Century* (Middletown, Conn., 1968), 108.

9. Kevin M. Sweeney. "Meetinghouses, Town Houses, and Churches, Changing Perceptions of Secular Space in Southern New England," *Winterthur* Portfolio, vol. 28, no. 1 (Spring 1993), 59.

10. Hugh Morrison, *Early American Architecture From the First Colonial Settlements to the National Period* (New York and Oxford, 1952), 79.

11. At Salem the new two-story town house (1677) also contained a schoolroom. Martha J. McNamara, "'In the face of the court . . .' Law, Commerce, and the Transformation of Public Space in Boston, 1650–1770," *Winterthur Portfolio*, 36:2/3, 125.

12. Ibid., 129.

13. Marcus Wiffen, "The Early County Courthouse of Virginia," *Journal of the Society of Architectural Historians*, vol. 18, March 1959, 3.

14. The Wren Building at the College of William and Mary in Williamsburg, or the Capitol there, may have been the source of this architectural feature.

15. Ibid. p. 51.

16. Patrick L. Pinnell, *Yale University, An Architectural Tour* (Princeton, 1999), 8.

17. Jefferson to James Madison, in John Reps, *Tidewater Towns*, 173. Also quoted in James D. Kornwolf, with the assistance of Georgiana W. Kornwolf, *Architecture and Town Planning in Colonial America*, 3 vols. (Baltimore & London: The Johns Hopkins University Press, 2002), vol. 3, 1406.

18. Sarah N. Randolph, *The Domestic Life of Thomas Jefferson* (Charlottesville, 1947) 80–81.

19. James Kornwolf, "So Good a Design," *The Colonial Campus of the College of William and Mary: Its History, Background, and Legacy* (Williamsburg, VA.: Joseph and Margaret Muscarelle Museum of Art, College of William and Mary, 1989).

20. The Roman Senate met on the Capitoline Hill in Rome, at the site of the Temple of Jupiter Capitolinus.

21. Kornwolf, vol. 3, 1407. Jefferson may well have been aware of the striking resemblance between the Capitoline Hill, where the Roman senate met, and the hill on which the Virginia Capitol was to be constructed.

22. Thomas Jefferson, *Notes on the State of Virginia*, Query XV, p. 278, TJ, *Writings*, 278, *Library of America*.

23. Ibid., 1408.

24. I am indebted to Mark Wenger of the Colonial Williamsburg Foundation, who generously discussed his research with me.

25. Jefferson, 20

26. Reps, *Tidewater Towns*, 275.

27. Fiske Kimball, *The Capitol of Virginia, A Landmark of American Architecture* (Richmond: The Library of Virginia, 2002), 41.

28. James D. Kornwolf, "Thomas Jefferson's Gift of Modern Architecture to Virginia and America," p. 14. This was delivered as the keynote address at the symposium *Jefferson and the Capitol of Virginia*, sponsored by the Library of Virginia and the Colonial Williamsburg Foundation, September 27–28, 2002. Quoted from the text of the speech that the author was kind enough to provide and allow me to quote.

29. Vincent Scully, *The New World's Vision of Household Gods & Sacred Places, American Art 1650–1914* (Boston, 1988), 71.

30. Samuel Gilman Brown, *The Works of Rufus Choate with a Memoir of His Life* (1862), vol. 1, 345.

31. Washington to the Commissioners, July 23, 1792, Fitzpatrick, ed., vol. 32, 93.

32. William C. Allen, *The History of the United States Capitol* (Washington D.C., 2001), 20.

33. Jefferson to Daniel Carroll, February 1, 1793, Padover, National Capital, 171.

34. The new City Hall in London, designed by Norman Foster and Associates, has a room for people to gather at the top of the building. Foster described it as a "living room" for the people of London.

35. George Washington to Bushrod Washington, November 9, 1787, in W. W. Abbot, editor, *The Papers of George Washington, Confederation Series, 5, February–December 1787* (Charlottesville & London: University Press of Virginia, 1997), 422–23.

36. Theodore Roosevelt, "Lincoln and Free Speech," The Great Adventure (vol. 19, of *The Works of Theodore Roosevelt*, 1926, national ed., chapter 7), 289.

37. *Presidential Addresses and State Papers of William Howard Taft* (1910) vol. 1, chapter 7, 82–83.

38. As late as 1804, Alexander Hamilton foiled a plan by powerful interests in New York to have

that state secede from the Union. This was a prime cause of Hamilton's fateful duel with Aaron Burr, who was one of the secessionist plotters.

39. Henry Russell Hitchcock and William Seale, "Notes on the Architecture," in Richard Pare, ed., *Court House, A Photographic Document* (New York, 1978), 165–66. They described courthouses as "local ornaments of the towns in which they stood."

40. Allan Greenberg, "Selecting a Courtroom Design," *Judicature*, vol. 59 (April 1976),422–28.

PART III: DEMOCRACY, ANTHROPOMORPHISM, AND ARCHITECTURE

1. Vincent Scully, *Architecture: The Natural and the Man Made* (New York, 1991), I.

2. Archibald MacLeish, "The American Cause," Nov. 20, 1940, in Macleish, *A Time to Act: Selected Addresses* (Boston, 1943), 115.

3. Henry James Jr., *Hawthorne* (Ithaca, 1997), 34. Quoted in Duncan Faherty, "A 'Game of Architectural Consequences': The American House and the Formation of National Identity, 1776-1858." (Ph.D. diss., City University of New York, 2003), 1–2.

4. A. B. Yehoshua, "Modern Democracy and the Novel," in Arthur M. Melzer, Jerry Weinberger, and M. Richard Zinman, eds., *Democracy & the Arts* (Ithaca, N.Y.: Cornell University Press, 1999), 42–43.

5. Alexis de Tocqueville, *Democracy in America*, vol 1, trans. and ed. Harvey Mansfield and Delba Winthrop (Chicago: University of Chicago Press, 2000), 274.

6. James Wilson, *Chisholm versus Georgia*. This was the first jurisdictional case brought before the new U.S. Supreme Court. Wilson, born in Scotland, was also a delegate to the Constitutional Convention.

7. Thomas Jefferson to Henry Lee, Monticello, May 8, 1825, Writings, ed. Merrill D. Peterson (New York: Literary Classics of the United States, 1984), 1501.

8. It was only after the revolution that professionally trained architects arrived in the United States. Their training was an informal apprenticeship system rather than a university education. The most noteworthy example is Benjamin Henry Latrobe, Jefferson's appointee as architect of the Capitol, who was trained in England in the office of Henry Holland. University training began in the later nineteenth century.

9. Anthropocentrism in this context is defined in the electronic Merriam-Webster's *Unabridged Dictionary* as "centering in human beings and interpreting the world in terms of human values and experiences."

10. Anthropomorphism is also evident in the architecture of other cultures such as in Bali and in Africa south of the Sahara. The unique contribution of the ancient Greeks was to relate it to democracy.

11. Geoffrey Scott, an English writer on architecture, described this as "transcribe[ing] ourselves in terms of architecture" as imaging, through the medium of empathy, that we are a building and parts of buildings like columns. This is explored in Scott's book, *The Architecture of Humanism: A Study in the History of Taste*, 2nd ed. (Gloucester, Mass.: P. Smith, 1965), 157–65.

12. In the electronic Merriam-Webster's *Unabridged Dictionary*, the etymology of the English word façade, together with the French façade and the Italian facciata, is derived from the Latin faccia or face.

13. Vitruvius, *The Ten Books on Architecture*, trans. Morris Hicky Morgan (New York: Dover Publications, 1960), 103.

14. Ibid., 103–4.

15. Francis Cranmer Penrose, *An Investigation of the Principles of Athenian Architecture or, The Results of a Survey Conducted Chiefly with Reference to the Optical Refinements Exhibited in the Construction of the Ancient Buildings of Athens* (1888), new and enlarged ed. (Washington: McGrath Publishing Company, 1973), 39–44.

16. Henry Millon, "The Architectural Theory of Francesco di Giorgio," *The Art Bulletin*, vol. 40, no. 3 (Sept., 1958), 257–61.

17. Francesco di Giorgio Martini, *Trattato di architettura: Il Codice Ashburnham 361 della Biblioteca Laurenziana*, ed. Pietro Marani, 2 vols., Florence, 1979, I, 3–4, lines 1–22. Quoted in Lawrence Lowic, "The meaning and Significance of the Human Analogy in Francesco di Giorgio's Trattato," *Journal of the Society of Architectural Historians*, vol. 42, no. 4, (Dec. 1983), 361.

18. Augustine, *City of God*, XIX.16.Quoted in Lowic, 363.

19. Lowic, 361.

20. Filarete's *Treatise on Architecture, Being the Treatise by Antonio di Piero Averlino, Known as Filarete*, trans. John R. Spencer., vol. I (New Haven, Conn.: Yale University Press, 1965), 10. Quoted in Alex T. Anderson, "On the Human Figure in Architectural Representation," *Journal of Architectural Education*, May 2002, 239.

21. David Summers, *Michelangelo and the Language of Art* (Princeton: Princeton University Press, 1981), 420.

22. Letter to an unknown prelate, ca. 1550 or 1560; quoted in Summers, 419.

23. Summers, 418.

24. In western architecture, the culmination of this preoccupation with systems of proportion may be Le Corbusier's remarkable Modulor. It combines the Fibonnaci series, the system of proportion used by the ancient Greeks, and the geometry of the Middle Ages and Renaissance. A building deigned using his red and blue scales ensures that every relationship in plan and elevation is related to the golden mean.

25. John Summerson, "The Mischievous Analogy," in *Heavenly Mansions and Other Essays on Architecture* (New York: W. W. Norton & Company, 1963), 203.

26. Summerson, 203.

27. Herman Melville, *Moby Dick; or, the Whale* (1851, reprinted by Modern Library: New York, 2000), 166–67.

28. Melville, 166.

29. Summerson, 203.

30. Albert Speer, interviewed by Robert Hughes, 1979, in "Albert Speer: Size Matters," Visions of Space, BBC-2, February 12, 2003.

31. Brian Ladd, *The Ghosts of Berlin* (Chicago: The University of Chicago Press, 1997), 135.

32. Some modernist architects, critics, and historians have asserted that classical architecture is a manifestation of fascism. This is based on ignorance and, more seriously, a form of visual blindness that ignored fascism's disdain for anthropomorphism and contextual architecture. Yes, Stalinist, Nazi, and modernist architects have used symmetry and classicizing formulae like columns and cornicelike features to complete the tops of buildings. Although they may be inspired by classical architecture, these features may also be part of the cannon of the architecture of other cultures and periods of history. The results are usually banal because incompatible philosophies do not generate architectural forms that relate well. This is why these architects' buildings lack visual coherence, anthropomorphic scale, and anthropocentric ideals. Ironically, the one modernist architect who has been able to merge modernism with classicism was Le Corbusier; and these same critics strive to ignore this aspect of his work. Both Sir John Summerson and Colin Rowe, however, noted that Le Corbusier's *five points of architecture* have a philosophical basis as a direct reaction to classical architectural principles. Le Corbusier is unique among modernists—except for Alvar Aalto and Mies van der Rohe—because his architecture stands so firmly on the shoulders of the past.

33. Speer acknowledged Hitler's dominant role in the design of the Grosse Halle, but that he was largely responsible for the rest of the plan for Berlin. See Barbara Miller Lane "Architects in Power: Politics and Ideology in the work of Ernst May and Albert Speer," *Journal of Interdisciplinary History*, vol. 17, no. 1, "The Evidence of Art: Images and Meaning in History" (Summer 1986), 298–99. In this paper, Professor Lane asserts that Speer was also influenced by the "Modern Movement," architecture in Europe and the United States in the 1930s, and by excavations at Assur, the early capital of the Assyrian Empire, in present day Iraq (pp. 302–03 and 305).

34. Götz Aly and Susanne Heim, *Architects of Annihilation: Auschwitz and the Logic of Destruction* (Princeton: Princeton University Press, 1991). At page 2, the authors describe the three forces that animated the "executive dynamism of National Socialist Germany [as being] generated by the interaction of: the abandonment of moral restraint, the pursuit of a nationalistic and expansionistic socialist utopia, and the emergence of a modern technocracy."

35. The Empire State Building has starred in nearly one hundred movies. These include *King Kong, Sleepless in Seattle*, and the two versions of *An Affair to Remember*.

36. *The Republic of Plato*, trans. Allan Bloom (New York: Basic Books, 1991), Book I, section 338 d, 16, and Book VIII, section 544 a, d, and e.

37. Carroll William Westfall, "The Humanity of Monumental Architecture," *American Arts Quarterly*, vol. XIX, (Winter 2002), 13.

38. Andy Logan, "Building For Glory," *The New Yorker* (October 21, 1961), 139.

39. Logan, 161–62.

40. Winston Weisman, "A New View of Skyscraper History," in *The Rise of an American Architecture*, ed. Edgar Kaufmann, Jr. (New York: Published in association with the Metropolitan Museum of Art by Praeger, 1970), 115–62.

41. Oscar Wilde, *An Ideal Husband*, Act 2, Scene 2.

42. T.S. Eliot, "Little Gidding," *Four Quartets* (London: Faber & Faber, 1959).

43. "Saving Fine Architecture," *The New York Times*, August 11, 1962, 11.

44. Norman Mailer and Vincent Scully, "Mailer versus Scully: On Contemporary Architecture," *Architectural Forum*, 120, 97.

45. Thomas Jefferson to George Wythe, Paris, August 13, 1786, *The Papers of Thomas Jefferson*, vol. 10, ed. Julian P. Boyd (Princeton: Princeton University Press, 1954), 244.

46. Women were not admitted as undergraduates in the College of Arts and Sciences until 1970. One remarkable woman managed to earn a degree in the late nineteenth century, and some women were permitted to take part in summer programs.

47. This remarkable analogy was made by Vincent Scully during a conversation with the author in 1974.

48. Jefferson to Latrobe, Monticello, July 12, 1812, Thomas Jefferson and the National Capitol, ed. Saul Padover (Washington, D.C.: United States Government Printing Office, 1946), 471.

49. Albert Sack, *Fine Points of American Furniture* (New York: Crown Books, 1993), 15.

INDEX

ILLUSTRATION CREDITS

BACK
COVER
& i-1 KEITH STANLEY/KESTAN.COM
i-2 LIBRARY OF CONGRESS, PRINTS AND PHO-
TOGRAPHS DIVISION [REPRODUCTION NUMBER,
LC-USZ62-115563]
i-3 © BETTMANN/CORBIS
i-4 © LEE SNIDER/PHOTO IMAGES/CORBIS
i-5 ALLAN GREENBERG
i-6 © EDIFICE/CORBIS
i-7 © ALEX SIEVERS/ WWW.SIEVERS.NL
i-8a, b KERSTIN MARTIN AND CECILIA WAHRNER
i-9 ALLAN GREENBERG
i-10 ROBERT BENSON
i-11 ALLAN GREENBERG
i-12 ALLAN GREENBERG
i-13 TIM BUCHMAN
i-14 TIM BUCHMAN
i-15 TIM HURSLEY
i-16 RAEL SLUTSKY
i-17 RICHARD CHEEK
1-1 ALLAN GREENBERG
1-2 © PARAMOUNT PICTURES/ VIACOM CONSUMER
PRODUCTS
1-3 THE NEW JERSEY STATE HISTORICAL SOCIETY
1-4 © BETTMANN/CORBIS
1-5 © RAYMOND GEHMAN/CORBIS
1-6 ALLAN GREENBERG
1-7 ALLAN GREENBERG
1-8 DRAWING OF THE OCTAGON HOUSE: LIBRARY OF
CONGRESS, PRINTS AND PHOTOGRAPHS DIVISION
[REPRODUCTION NUMBER, LC-USZ62-60172]
DRAWING OF THE LOUVRE: COURTESY OF
THE KYOTO UNIVERSITY DIGITAL LIBRARY
1-9 DEL. TOMAS RAMIREZ
1-10 ALLAN GREENBERG
1-11 © BRIAN VANDEN BRINK
COVER
& 1-12 HISTORIC AMERICAN BUILDINGS SURVEY
[REPRODUCTION NUMBER, HABS PA,46-VALFO,1-28]
1-13 © ROMAN SOUMAR/CORBIS
1-14 ALLAN GREENBERG
1-15 HISTORIC AMERICAN BUILDINGS SURVEY [REPRO-
DUCTION NUMBER, HABS PA,51-PHILA,15-25]
1-16 HISTORIC AMERICAN BUILDINGS SURVEY
[REPRODUCTION NUMBER, HABS SC,10,CHAR,2-4]
1-17 TIM BUCHMAN
1-18 © DAVE G. HOUSER/CORBIS
1-19 TIM BUCHMAN
1-20 ALLAN GREENBERG
1-21 ALLAN GREENBERG
1-22 © ROYALTY-FREE CORBIS
1-23 © RUGGERO VANNI/CORBIS
1-24 ©2005 CAROLYN L. BATES - CAROLYNBATES.COM
1-25a TIM BUCHMAN
1-25b BETTY LANGLEY, *The City and Country Builder's and
Workman's Treasury of Designs* (London, 1750).
1-26 DAVID OTTENSTEIN
1-27 ROBERT LAUTMAN
1-28 HISTORIC AMERICAN BUILDINGS SURVEY
[REPRODUCTION NUMBER, HABS VA,2-CHAR.V,1-43]
1-29 ROBERT LAUTMAN
1-30 HISTORIC AMERICAN BUILDINGS SURVEY
[REPRODUCTION NUMBER, HABS VA,2-CHAR.V,1-22]
1-31 ROBERT LAUTMAN
1-32 ROBERT LAUTMAN
1-33 MONTICELLO/THOMAS JEFFERSON FOUNDATION, INC.
1-34 ROBERT LAUTMAN
1-35 ROBERT LAUTMAN
1-36a, b DEL. ERIKA ALBRIGHT
1-37 DEL. ERIKA ALBRIGHT
1-38 MOUNT VERNON LADIES' ASSOCIATION
1-39 MOUNT VERNON LADIES' ASSOCIATION
1-40 TIM BUCHMAN

1-41a, b DEL. ROB McCLENNAN
1-42 DEL. BOB COLARRUSO
1-43 TIM BUCHMAN
1-44 TIM BUCHMAN
1-45 TIM BUCHMAN
1-46 TIM BUCHMAN
1-47 DEL. SLADE ELKINS
1-48 DEL. WILLIAM BOURQUE
1-49 MOUNT VERNON LADIES ASSOCIATION
1-50 TIM BUCHMAN
1-51 DEL. SLADE ELKINS
1-52 TIM BUCHMAN
1-53 MOUNT VERNON LADIES ASSOCIATION
1-54a BRIDGEMAN ART LIBRARY
1-54b DEL. TOMAS RAMIREZ
1-55 © JON R. HOLMQUIST
1-56 © FREE AGENTS LIMITED/CORBIS
1-57 © LEE SNIDER/PHOTO IMAGES/CORBIS
1-58 © LEE SNIDER/PHOTO IMAGES/CORBIS
1-59 RICHARD CHEEK
1-60 ALLAN GREENBERG

2-1 ROBERT LAUTMAN
2-2 1749 PLYMOUTH COURTHOUSE MUSEUM
2-3 HISTORIC AMERICAN BUILDINGS SURVEY [REPRO-
DUCTION NUMBER, HABS MASS,5,MARB,3-2]
2-4 © G.E. KIDDER SMITH/CORBIS
2-5 © LEE SNIDER/PHOTO IMAGES/CORBIS
2-6 HISTORIC AMERICAN BUILDINGS SURVEY [REPRO-
DUCTION NUMBER, HABS CONN,5-NEWHA,1-4]
2-7a THE BOSTONIAN SOCIETY
2-7b HISTORIC AMERICAN BUILDINGS SURVEY [REPRO-
DUCTION NUMBER, HABS HABS MASS,13-BOST,51-1]
2-8 © LEE SNIDER/PHOTO IMAGES/CORBIS
2-9 NORTH CAROLINA STATE ARCHIVES
2-10 HISTORIC AMERICAN BUILDINGS SURVEY
[REPRODUCTION NUMBER, HABS VA,66,EAST,1-1]
2-11 THOMAS NOBLE/ALLAN GREENBERG ARCHITECT
2-12 THOMAS NOBLE/ALLAN GREENBERG ARCHITECT
2-13 HISTORIC AMERICAN BUILDINGS SURVEY [REPRO-
DUCTION NUMBER, HABS ME,16,YORK,V1-11]
2-14 © LEE SNIDER/PHOTO IMAGES/CORBIS
2-15 HARVARD UNIVERSITY ARCHIVES
2-16 © BETTMANN/CORBIS
2-17 THE HISTORICAL SOCIETY OF PENNSYLVANIA/
G.W. SMITH
2-18 MATTHEW WIGGLESWORTH/ALLAN GREENBERG
ARCHITECT
2-19 OHIO HISTORICAL SOCIETY
2-20 © WILLIAM BOYCE/CORBIS
2-21 © CORBIS
2-22 JOHN O. PETERS/VIRGINIA BAR ASSOCIATION
2-23 ALLAN GREENBERG
2-24 HISTORIC AMERICAN BUILDINGS SURVEY [REPRO-
DUCTION NUMBER, HABS CONN,8,BROOK,3-1]
2-25 HISTORIC AMERICAN BUILDINGS SURVEY
[REPRODUCTION NUMBER, HABS VA,17,BOGR,2-2]
2-26 WADE ZIMMERMAN
2-27 HISTORIC AMERICAN BUILDINGS SURVEY
[REPRODUCTION NUMBER, HABS AK,19-EGL,1-E-3]
2-28 CARTE POSTALE, NELS / LOGO
2-29 © CORBIS
2-30 © ARCHIVO ICONOGRAFICO, S.A./CORBIS
2-31 © RICHARD T. NOWITZ/CORBIS
2-32 © DAVE G. HOUSER/CORBIS
2-33 MASSACHUSETTS HISTORICAL SOCIETY
2-34 HISTORIC AMERICAN BUILDINGS SURVEY
[REPRODUCTION NUMBER, HABS VA,44,RICH,9-53]
2-35 © BUDDY MAYS/CORBIS
2-36 MARYLAND HISTORICAL SOCIETY, BALTIMORE,
MARYLAND
2-37 & p. 204 VALENTINE RICHMOND HISTORY CENTER
2-38 PRIVATE COLLECTION OF AUTHOR, ARTIST
UNKOWN
2-39 THOMAS NOBLE/ALLAN GREENBERG ARCHITECT
2-40 © WWW.CONSULTWEBS.COM

2-41 HISTORIC AMERICAN BUILDINGS SURVEY [REPRO-
DUCTION NUMBER, HABS PA,51-PHILA,328-9]
2-42 MARY ANN SULLIVAN/BLUFFTON UNIVERSITY
2-43 ROBERT LAUTMAN
2-44 HISTORIC AMERICAN BUILDINGS SURVEY
[REPRODUCTION NUMBER, HABS GA,123,AUG,11-1]
ENDS
& 2-45 ATHENAEUM OF PHILADELPHIA
2-46 LIBRARY OF VIRGINIA
2-47 HISTORIC AMERICAN BUILDINGS SURVEY
[REPRODUCTION NUMBER, HABS VA,44-RICH,9-]
2-48 © BETTMAN/CORBIS
2-49 WILLIAM CLIFT, SEAGRAM COUNTY COURT HOUSE
ARCHIVES, LIBRARY OF CONGRESS, [LC-S35-WC24-3]
2-50 PRINTS & DRAWINGS COLLECTION,
THE OCTAGON, THE MUSEUM OF THE AMERICAN
ARCHITECTURAL FOUNDATION, WASHINGTON, DC
2-51 LIBRARY OF CONGRESS, PRINTS AND PHO-
TOGRAPHS DIVISION [REPRODUCTION NUMBER,
LC-USZC4-112]
2-52 ©STAPLETON COLLECTION/CORBIS
2-53 © THE METROPOLITAN MUSEUM OF ART, PUR-
CHASE, JOSEPH PULITZER BEQUEST, 1942 (42.138)
2-54 AVERY ARCHITECTURAL AND FINE ARTS LIBRARY,
COLUMBIA UNIVERSITY
2-55 AVERY ARCHITECTURAL AND FINE ARTS LIBRARY,
COLUMBIA UNIVERSITY
2-56 LIBRARY OF CONGRESS, PRINTS AND PHO-
TOGRAPHS DIVISION [REPRODUCTION
NUMBER,LC-USZC4-260]
2-57 THE NEW JERSEY HISTORICAL SOCIETY
2-58 LIBRARY OF CONGRESS, GEOGRAPHY AND
MAP DIVISION
2-59 ARCHITECT OF THE CAPITOL
2-60 © MARK THIESSEN/CORBIS
2-61 ALLAN GREENBERG
2-62 © ANGELO HORNAK/CORBIS
2-63 © BETTMANN/CORBIS
2-64 © JOSEPH SOHM; CHROMOSOHM INC./CORBIS
2-65 AVERY ARCHITECTURAL AND FINE ARTS LIBRARY,
COLUMBIA UNIVERSITY
2-66 © PHIL SCHERMEISTER/CORBIS
2-67 © LAKE COUNTY MUSEUM/CORBIS
2-68 © JOSEPH SOHM; CHROMOSOHM INC./CORBIS
2-69 CHET BURAK PHOTOGRAPHY
2-70 NORTH DAKOTA STATE GOVERNMENT, FACILITY
MANAGEMENT DIVISION
2-71 © CORBIS
2-72 INSTRUCTIONAL TECHNOLOGY DIVISION OF NCDPI
2-73 ALLAN GREENBERG
2-74 © DAVE G. HOUSER/CORBIS
2-75 RICHARD PARE, SEAGRAM COUNTY COURT HOUSE
ARCHIVES, LIBRARY OF CONGRESS, [LC-S35-WC24-3]
2-76 CORBIS COMPETITION FOR THE NEW YORK
COURTHOUSE, COURTHOUSE BOARD OF
NEW YORK COUNTY
2-77 © LAKE COUNTY MUSEUM/
2-78 HISTORIC AMERICAN BUILDINGS SURVEY
[REPRODUCTION NUMBER, HABS NY,28,ROCH,15-2]
2-79 PAUL ROCHELEAU
2-80 DEL. ALLAN GREENBERG
2-81 ALLAN GREENBERG
2-82 HISTORIC AMERICAN BUILDINGS SURVEY
[REPRODUCTION NUMBER, HABS DC,WASH,136-8]
2-83 ALLAN GREENBERG
2-84 HISTORIC AMERICAN BUILDINGS SURVEY [REPRO-
DUCTION NUMBER, HABS UTAH,20,SPRICI, 4-1]
2-85 ALLAN GREENBERG
2-86 THE MUSEUM OF THE CITY OF NEW YORK
2-87 MUSEUM OF HISTORY & INDUSTRY, SEATTLE
2-88 JIM BARTSCH PHOTOGRAPHER

3-01 PHOTOGRAPH BY WILL BROWN/UNITED STATES
DEPARTMENT OF STATE
3-02 © VANNI ARCHIVE/CORBIS
3-03 © RICHARD GLOVER/CORBIS

3-04 HISTORIC AMERICAN BUILDINGS SURVEY
[REPRODUCTION NUMBER, HABS VA,44,RICH.V,3-13]
3-05a ALLAN GREENBERG
3-05b ALLAN GREENBERG
3-06 BIBLIOTECA MEDICEA LAURENZIANA
3-07a © ROYALTY-FREE/CORBIS
3-07b BIBLIOTECA MEDICEA LAURENZIANA
3-08a © WOLFGANG KAEHLER/CORBIS
3-08b DEL. WILLIAM BORQUE
3-09 © JACK FIELDS/CORBIS
3-10 ALLAN GREENBERG
3-11 BIBLIOTECA MEDICEA LAURENZIANA
3-12 JOHN SHUTE, *The First and Chief Groundes of Architecture
Used in All the Ancient and Famous Monymentes* (1563).
3-13 ROBERT LAUTMAN
3-14 DEPARTMENT OF SPECIAL COLLECTIONS,
STANFORD UNIVERSITY LIBRARY
3-15a BIBLIOTECA NAZIONALE DI FIRENZE
3-15b HENRY MILLON
3-16 BIBLIOTECA NAZIONALE DI FIRENZE
3-17 ALLAN GREENBERG
3-18 THOMAS NOBLE/ALLAN GREENBERG ARCHITECT
3-19 © PIERRE VAUTHEY/CORBIS SYGMA
3-20a © BOARD OF TRUSTEES, NATIONAL GALLERY
OF ART, WASHINGTON, DC
3-20b ARCHITECT OF THE CAPITOL
3-21a WADE ZIMMERMAN
3-21b ROBERT LAUTMAN
3-22a ALLAN GREENBERG
3-22b EDWARD WARREN HOAK AND WILLIS HUMPHREY
CHURCH
3-22c ALLAN GREENBERG
3-23 © COLIN HOSKINS; CORDAIY PHOTO LIBRARY
LTD/CORBIS
3-24 TASHYA LEYMAN
3-25 ULLSTEIN BILD
3-26 DEL. TOMAS RAMIREZ
3-27 ULLSTEIN BILD
3-28 ULLSTEIN BILD
3-29a © 2005 ARTISTS RIGHTS SOCIETY (ARS),
NEW YORK/ADAGP, PARIS/FLC
3-29b © 2005 ARTISTS RIGHTS SOCIETY (ARS),
NEW YORK/ADAGP, PARIS/FLC
3-29c © 2005 ARTISTS RIGHTS SOCIETY (ARS),
NEW YORK/ADAGP, PARIS/FLC
3-29d © 2005 ARTISTS RIGHTS SOCIETY (ARS),
NEW YORK/ADAGP, PARIS/FLC
3-30 THOMAS AIRVIEWS COLLECTION
3-31a WADE ZIMMERMAN
3-31b WADE ZIMMERMAN
3-32 TRI-STAR / THE KOBAL COLLECTION / BRUCE
McBROOM
3-33 © G.E. KIDDER SMITH/CORBIS
3-34a © KEVIN FLEMING/CORBIS
3-34b PICTURE COLLECTION, THE BRANCH LIBRARIES,
THE NEW YORK PUBLIC LIBRARY, ASTOR, LENOX
AND TILDEN FOUNDATIONS
3-35 BIBLIOTECA MEDICEA LAURENZIANA
3-36 BERRY COLLEGE, OFFICE OF PUBLIC RELATIONS
3-37 AVERY ARCHITECTURAL AND FINE ARTS LIBRARY,
COLUMBIA UNIVERSITY
3-38 WADE ZIMMERMAN
3-39 GLENN GLASSER
3-40 © ANGELO HORNAK/CORBIS
3-41 © BETTMANN/CORBIS
3-42 © ALAN SCHEIN PHOTOGRAPHY/CORBIS
3-43 LIBRARY OF CONGRESS, PRINTS AND
PHOTOGRAPHS DIVISION [REPRODUCTION
NUMBER,LC-G612-T01-19735]
3-44 WADE ZIMMERMAN
3-45 LIBRARY OF CONGRESS, PRINTS AND
PHOTOGRAPHS DIVISION [REPRODUCTION
NUMBER,LC-USZ62-84014]
3-46a ALLAN GREENBERG
3-46b GLENN GLASSER
3-47a, b PHOTOGRAPH © MUSEUM OF FINE ARTS BOSTON

COLLE   FOR ORPHANS